Commercial and Investment Real Estate: Tools of the Trade

Edward S. Smith, Jr. CREI, ITI, CIC, RECS, GREEN, MICP

A Kaplan Real Estate Education Company

This publication is designed to provide accurate and authoritative information in regard to the subject matter covered. It is sold with the understanding that the publisher is not engaged in rendering legal, accounting, or other professional advice. If legal advice or other expert assistance is required, the services of a competent professional should be sought.

President: Dr. Andrew Temte
Chief Learning Officer: Dr. Tim Smaby
Vice President, Real Estate Education: Asha Alsobrooks
Development Editor: Adam Bissen

COMMERCIAL AND INVESTMENT REAL ESTATE: TOOLS OF THE TRADE
©2012 Kaplan, Inc.
Published by DF Institute, Inc., d/b/a Dearborn Real Estate Education
332 Front St. S., Suite 501
La Crosse, WI 54601

All rights reserved. The text of this publication, or any part thereof, may not be reproduced in any manner whatsoever without written permission from the publisher.

Printed in the United States of America
First revision, February 2014
ISBN: 978-1-4277-3165-4 / 1-4277-3165-9
PPN: 1520-7203

contents

about the author vi
introduction vii

Chapter 1 — Commercial Real Estate Opportunities 1

Key Terms 2
Types of Commercial Buildings and Properties 2
The Business Cycle 3
Types of Commercial Customers and Clients 3
Gathering General Property Information 9
Commercial Inventory 13
Review Questions 14

Chapter 2 — All About Office Buildings 15

Key Terms 15
Classifications of Office Buildings 16
Office Building Considerations 18
Lease Clauses 21
Office Buildings as Investments 24
Office Building Checklist 25
Case Study: Using the Office Building Checklist 27
Review Questions 29

Chapter 3 — Retail Properties 30

Key Terms 30
Retail Buildings 31
Anchor Tenants 31
Other Retail Terms 32
Retail Specialty Businesses 33
Site Considerations and Concerns 34
Special Retail Lease 35
Retail Building Checklist 37
Review Questions 39

Chapter 4 — Industrial Buildings and Their Physical Characteristics 40

Key Terms 40
Site Inspections 41
Building Features 42
Environmental Issues 44
Marketing of Industrial Properties 45
Case Study: Industrial Building Checklist 48
Review Questions 49

Chapter 5 — Introduction to Financial Analysis 50

Key Terms 50
Investment Analysis Worksheet 51
Case Study: Financial Analysis of Mountain View Mini Mall 54
Review Questions 59

Chapter 6 — The Value of Investments 60

Key Terms 60
Investment Strategies 61
Comparison of Investment Methods 61
CCIM—Certified Commercial Investment Member 63
Review Questions 65

Chapter 7 — Forecasting Cash Flows 66

Key Terms 66
Current Year Analysis 67
Case Study: Small Office Building 67
Case Study: Mr. Smith's Office 67
The Spreadsheet 74
Returns on Investments 80
Market Value 81
Reality Check: The Buyer's Perspective 83
Evaluating Assumptions 85
Commercial Brokerage 86
Review Questions 87

Chapter 8 — Depreciation and Cash Flow After Taxes 88

Key Terms 88
Depreciation or Cost Recovery 89
Review Questions 95

Chapter 9 — Selling Property: Capital Gains Taxes and 1031 Exchanges 96

Key Terms 97
Capital Gains Taxes 97
Sale of a Primary/Principal Residence 97
Sale of Commercial and investment Property 98
1031 Exchanges 101
Review Questions 104

Chapter 10 — Dealing with Other Brokers 105

Key Terms 105
Commission Splits 106
Co-Broke Agreements 108
Showing Records and Activity Reports 111
Review Questions 116

Chapter 11 — Marketing for Success 117

Key Term 117
The Internet 118
Traditional Forms of Advertising 118
Database Marketing 121
Property Marketing Plan 124
Building Your Business 126
Conclusion 127
Review Questions 128

Appendix A — Commercial Real Estate Online Resources 129

Web Sites 129
Newsgroups 130
Organizational Sites 131
Real Estate News 131

answer key 132
glossary 137
index 140

about the author

Edward S. Smith Jr. is a New York State–licensed real estate broker, specializing in commercial and investment real estate, with many years of brokerage experience. He previously owned his own brokerage firm and then served as a "consultant to the trade" and is currently a regional director for Coldwell Banker Commercial NRT.

Smith is an Instructor Training Institute (ITI) graduate with over 13 years' experience teaching real estate courses. He has developed seven commercial continuing education courses. He is also the author of five books on commercial and investment real estate and has had over one hundred articles published on these subjects.

He is past president and currently serves on the board of directors of the New York State Commercial Association of REALTORS® (NYSCAR), the Metro-Long Island Chapter of NYSCAR, and the Long Island Commercial Network (LICN).

Visit the author's Web site at *www.commercialed.com*.

introduction

To renew a license in many states, real estate professionals are required to take continuing education (CE) courses. Early in my career, there were no CE courses related to commercial and investment real estate. But as my business and personal experience evolved, I was encouraged to write one. Commercial real estate courses proved to be very popular, and I found myself teaching them for several REALTOR® boards and schools. This started my expanded career as a real estate author and instructor.

In this book, I will share lessons I have learned over almost four decades in the field to give you, the student, a full understanding of commercial and investment real estate. This segment of the real estate business has its own language. You will learn the many words and terms that make up the commercial jargon. This process will begin by studying the different types of commercial properties and customers. You will also begin to understand the numbers and formulas used to value properties and show investment returns. This book includes plenty of examples, case studies, and forms to help you gather information and evaluate opportunities.

When we talk about investment properties, the key question is often "what's the bottom line?" Throughout the book, this question can be examined from various perspectives—for example, if a property is purchased solely with cash or through financing. But before we can calculate a bottom line, we must also consider what is left each year after taxes and other expenses are paid. This book will explore investments that may be tax-deductable and how to perform these calculations. Eventually properties may be sold, possibly triggering capital gains taxes. We will also look at the rules and ramifications of capital gains taxes and introduce the possibility of a 1031 exchange.

This book covers the full gamut of real estate activity—from evaluation to investment to marketing. I spent decades learning and teaching the material in this book, and I hope to present it in a step-by-step manner that you'll find informative and easy to understand.

chapter one

Commercial Real Estate Opportunities

overview

The two basic types of commercial customers and clients are users and investors. Each type focuses on different reasons for purchasing property. Sometimes, the reasons overlap and we have user-investor customers and clients. When you add to this the many different types of commercial and investment properties, you can see all the brokerage opportunities available in the commercial real estate field.

The information needed to sell and lease commercial and investment property falls into several categories: ownership information, specific details of the building or space, and financial data. In addition, it is necessary to recognize the role of other professionals who will be part of the transaction. This and subsequent chapters will address what you need to know about each of these areas. ∎

learning objectives

After completing this chapter, you will be able to

- identify the primary types of commercial properties,
- identify various types of commercial customers,
- describe the advantage of buying rather than leasing properties,
- describe how to use the CAP rate formula to determine market value,
- describe tenant-buyer representation,
- understand the value of third-party advisers, and
- describe the value of using a property checklist.

Key Terms

annual debt service
build to suit
capitalization (CAP) rate
income approach
exit strategy
net operating income (NOI)
return on investment (ROI)

Types of Commercial Property and Customers

There are four primary types of commercial properties:

- Office
- Industrial
- Retail
- Apartments

Each type includes many kinds of buildings:

- Office
    - Highrise or lowrise
    - Professional
    - Medical
    - Office condo
- Industrial
    - Warehouses, distribution centers
    - Factories
    - Manufacturing plants
    - Research and development (R&D)
- Retail
    - Free-standing store
    - Strip centers
    - Shopping centers—malls
    - Outlet centers
- Apartment
    - Multifamily houses
    - Apartment buildings
    - Mixed-use buildings

Other commercial properties are unique and are not found within these classifications (e.g., schools, churches, hotels, and assisted living facilities). Land can also be considered a commercial property. It is either classified as a residential subdivision or, depending on its potential use, is included in one of the previously listed categories. This chapter will look at each group of commercial properties in detail.

Kinds of Commercial Buildings

The opportunities for commercial business are legion. Think about all the different types of buildings and properties we see every day. A quick list of some properties might include the following:

- Gas stations
- Fast food

- Drug stores
- Banks
- Golf courses
- Marinas
- Auto uses
- Outside storage
- Parking garages
- Restaurants
- Businesses for sale
- Neighborhood strips of stores
- Nursing or adult homes
- Outlet centers

Remember: Anything we can sell, we can also lease.

Generally, in residential real estate, one customer is looking to purchase one home and after you sell that person a home, little additional business remains to be done. Granted, that customer might move again or refer business to you, but generally the sales opportunity ends there—one customer, one sale.

The many types of commercial properties provide multiple opportunities to conduct numerous transactions. In addition, and perhaps more important, commercial brokerage is redundant. Expired leases provide opportunities to again service the client. Investors might buy additional buildings. Commercial customers can be yours for life; you will do business with them over and over again. Think about it. If a customer signs a five-year lease for a store, do you have the opportunity to service that customer when the lease expires? If you sell an investor a good investment building this year, do you think that investor may buy another building next year or sooner?

The Business Cycle

It is said that every three to five years "something" occurs with every business. The business is either growing and needs more space (or additional locations), or it needs to downsize or close. These cyclical events offer opportunities for commercial real estate specialists. It is important to maintain relationships with your customers and periodically inquire into how their businesses are doing.

You can help your customers in several ways. Perhaps you leased a store to a client for five years, and after two years, you find he is doing really well and needs more space. You can help the client find that new location and either sublease the current space or work with the landlord to find a new tenant. This is just one example of how following the business cycle can lead to increased business.

Types of Commercial Customers and Clients

User Customers

Customers are considered users when they intend to operate their business from a building they rent or buy. They will occupy all or a portion of that property. Their decision is based on what is best for their business, and the primary consideration is location, location, location. Will their business flourish there? These customers are space-driven. Another major concern is the size of the space—does it match their requirements? One would not usually lease or purchase more space than what is needed, although some thought may be given to growth and future expansion.

Users will also question whether the defined market area provides the services needed by their business. They will evaluate the defined market area's employment pool. Can the necessary workers be found and hired at a wage rate conducive to the business? Transportation is also an important issue. Is mass transit available to help employees travel to work? If the business produces products (e.g., a manufacturing plant), is the necessary truck or rail access readily available?

User clients like to follow new markets. They will go where the business will be. For example, if a new residential community is being developed, there will be a need for local service stores, perhaps a dry cleaner, coffee shop, stationery shop, or video store.

User Investors

User customers may buy a building larger than their needs, intending to rent the extra space to other tenants. The income from these rental units might effectively reduce the buyer's cost of owning the building. This reduction of expenses through positive cash flow is, in essence, a profit. When this cash flow (profit) is compared with the cost of buying the building (or the down payment), a return on investment is shown. The user customer has now become an investor too.

Example:
The User Investor

A user finds what seems to be an ideal location for a business. The small building has a 2,000-square-foot retail space on the ground floor and two apartments on the second floor. The owner would like $15 per square foot (PSF) to rent the store, or $30,000 per year. The owner would also be willing to sell the building for $420,000. All the tenants pay their own utilities and a proportionate share of real estate taxes. The two apartments account for $12,000 a year in net rental income.

The user investor may buy the building and reduce the cost paid for the space occupied by the user investor. To illustrate this, a few assumptions are needed. Assume the building is purchased for $420,000 with a down payment of $160,000. A mortgage can be obtained for $260,000 with a 15-year term, 8 percent fixed interest rate and a monthly payment due of $2,485 or $29,816 as annual debt service (see Figure 1.1).

After purchasing the building, the income from the apartments ($12,000) will be used to pay part of the annual debt service. The rent from the store (which the buyer will occupy) will be used to pay the remaining balance of the annual mortgage expense $17,816. By becoming a user investor, the buyer effectively reduces the anticipated leasing expense of $30,000 a year for the store to $17,816 (see Figure 1.2).

Also, this user investor has now invested $160,000 into the building. The savings in rent can be considered a return on that investment. An investor's return on investment (ROI) is expressed as a percentage of profit based on the initial investment, which in this case is the down payment.

By buying the building, the user has become a user investor, has effectively reduced the rent by $12,184, and has a 7.6 percent return on the investment (see Figure 1.3).

Figure 1.1 | User Investor Purchase Terms

Cost of building	$420,000
Down payment	$160,000
Mortgage amount (15 year term, 8% Interest rate)	$260,000
Monthly payment	$2,485
Annual debt service	$29,816

Investor Clients

Investors are profit driven because they are primarily concerned with the return on their investment dollars. "What is the bottom line?" is apt to be their first question. When evaluating a purchase, they look at the current income the property produces and consider future income. Perhaps old leases, soon to expire, are charging under-market rates. Perhaps the building could produce more revenue if it were modernized or rehabbed.

Having a strong rent roll helps create a solid **net operating income (NOI)**. This is the figure that investors use to calculate a building's value. In its simplest terms, the net operating income is the monies left after all the owner's operating expenses are subtracted from the gross operating income of the property.

Gross operating income − Owner's operating expenses = Net operating income

Another concern of investors is stability. Will the present income continue? Will the tenants continue to occupy the property? Will there be an increase in vacancies? How long might it take to replace a tenant? What are the local vacancy rates? Investors will research the area to find out what kind of vacancy exists in comparable buildings. They will also look at area trends. For example, is any new construction (i.e., new competition) planned in the area?

Wise investors look at the big picture. These customers will examine every potential purchase for

- immediate value,
- cash flow over time, and
- future value.

Real estate investors should also develop an **exit strategy**, calculating how long they intend to hold the investment and when they intend to sell it. How much should the property appreciate during the holding period? For how much will they be able to sell the building in x number of years? One strategy is to buy it cheap, fix it up, lease at market rates, and sell relatively quickly. Other investors never sell. Still others may finance for over 10 years or more—a typical finance

Figure 1.2 | Effective Rent

Annual debt service	$29,816
Less apartment income	− $12,000
Effective store rent	$17,816

Figure 1.3 | Return on Investment

Rental of space (2,000 sq. ft. @ $15/sq. ft.)	$30,000
Reduced rent required as a result of purchase	$17,816
Rent savings (return on investment)	$12,184
Initial investment (down payment)	$160,000
Return on investment %	7.6%

$$\frac{\text{Rent savings}}{\text{Initial investment}} \quad \frac{\$12,184}{\$160,000} = 0.076 \ (7.6\%)$$

plan is 15 years—and dispose of the property as soon as the building's mortgage is paid off.

Capitalization rate. Previously, we looked at the return on investment for a user investor, based on rent savings. Pure investors will look at the net operating income of properties and determine how to realize the return they desire if they purchase the property, or what the property is worth to them. Sellers often ask a similar question of brokers: "What is my property worth?"

A **capitalization (CAP) rate** is used to determine market value. It is based on the premise that a correlation exists between the income a property produces and its value. The CAP rate can be looked at as a desired profit percentage for an investor. By using a CAP rate, a market value can be determined. This concept is also called the **income approach** to determining value.

CAP rates are based on local economies. They vary geographically and change frequently. From a practical point of view, they are a reflection of what investors in that particular area, at that particular time, are willing to accept as a return on their investments. When one applies for a mortgage loan on commercial and investment properties, the bank requires an income and expense statement of the property, which shows the net operating income. They also require a copy of the contract. Dividing the NOI by the sales price shows the ROI or CAP rate for that deal. Banks see patterns of acceptable return rates for investors and publish these CAP rates for each category of property. Brokers attain this information and use it to determine current market values.

Example:

Using CAP Rate to Calculate Market Value

Market value equals the net operating income (NOI) divided by the CAP rate.

$$\text{Value} = \frac{\text{NOI}}{\text{Rate}}$$

- A property has an NOI of $50,000.
- The investor's desired profit percentage—CAP rate—is 10 percent.
- What is the market value of the property?

$$\$50,000 \div 0.10\ (10\%) = \$500,000 \text{ market value}$$

$$\frac{\$50,000\,(\text{NOI})}{0.10\,(\text{rate})} = \$500,000\,(\text{value})$$

What are we saying? An investor will pay $500,000 for a building. The net operating income of the building is $50,000; this gives the investor a 10 percent return on the investment. (Note: Financing costs are not being considered at this time.)

Example:

Solving for the CAP Rate

The capitalization (CAP) rate equals the net operating income divided by the market value.

$$\text{CAP rate} = \frac{\text{NOI}}{\text{Value}}$$

A property has an NOI of $60,000. A buyer offers to purchase it for $500,000. What CAP rate does the buyer seek?

Remember: NOI divided by the value equals the CAP rate. Therefore,

$$\frac{\$60,000\ (\text{NOI})}{\$500,000\ (\text{value})} = 0.12\ (12\%)\ \text{CAP rate}$$

Example:

CAP Rate Problem A

A property is priced at $750,000 and has an NOI of $67,000. What CAP rate is being offered?

To solve for the CAP rate:

$$\frac{\text{NOI}}{\text{Value}} = \text{CAP rate} \qquad \frac{\$67,000}{\$750,000} = 0.893\ (9\%)$$

The CAP rate (rounded) is 9 percent.

> ### Example:
>
> **CAP Rate Problem B**
>
> An investor wants to sell her building. She advises you that she has an NOI of $48,000 and will offer the property at an 11 percent CAP. At what price do you market the building?
>
> To solve for market value:
>
> $$\frac{NOI}{Rate} = Value \qquad \frac{\$48,000}{0.11} = \$436,363$$
>
> The market value may be rounded to $436,000.

Developers

Another type of commercial investor is the developer. These investors purchase a property, often land, and construct (i.e., develop) a building for a specific customer. This practice is known as **build to suit**. Often a developer will buy land and then seek a national tenant to lease a building that the developer will construct for the tenant in accordance with the tenant's plans and specifications. Other times, the developer may put up a new office building or a strip of stores or other type of income-producing property on "spec"—speculation that when completed (or before) the developer will successfully lease the space. The developer-investor may then sell the property or hold it for a period.

Tenant-Buyer Representatives

Commercial real estate specialists may represent customers who are seeking to buy or lease properties; in these cases, they may act as buyer brokers or tenant representatives. Specific agreements are required for these arrangements. Tenant representation will often involve national companies that want to expand into a new market area, and it can involve finding multiple locations.

The nature of the assignment is defined in the broker's agreement, which will include a specific geographic area or defined market area in which the tenant wishes to locate. The agreement usually states the rate of commission to be paid to the broker for various services rendered. It usually states that the broker first look to the property owner to pay the commission. If, however, the broker is not being paid at all by the owner or not being paid a full commission by the owner, the tenant will pay the commission or the difference in the commission amount. A tenant representation agreement further defines broker and client obligations.

Often these agreements have a confidentiality clause stipulating that the broker cannot disclose the identity of the client until after a transaction is agreed to—the premise being that if the owner knew the identity of the national client, the rental or sale price could be inflated.

Gathering General Property Information

Ownership Information

In gathering data about property ownership, start with a complete description of the property's location. This includes the following location information:

- Street address, town, state, and zip code
- Closest cross street
- County
- Deed description (i.e., tax map, section, lot and block, or parcel number, etc.)

Most of this information may seem relatively obvious, but why the cross street? Many clients use computer programs to generate market information and demographic reports, and these usually require an address and a cross street. It is good to be able to provide the information to your customers before they ask for it.

Who actually owns the property? Is it an individual or a corporation? If it is a corporation, who are the officers or principals? Often the property owner does not work on the site, and so a separate address for the owner may be necessary. The owner may even live out of area. In either case, the name and phone numbers of a contact person who will show the property will be required. These facts are summarized by the following information:

- Owner:
    - Name or company
    - Name of principal, if company owned
    - Owner's address, town, state, zip code
    - Phone, fax, and e-mail
- Contact to show:
    - Name
    - Phone, fax, and e-mail

Third-Party Advisers

At the time the listing is taken, it is important to ask owners for the name of their attorney. In some states, residential real estate transactions consist of three steps: first, the home is listed; then, a sales price is agreed upon; and then the parties choose attorneys to represent them in closing the sale. In other states, real estate licensees issue residential contracts and close transactions (with or without the parties having legal representation). But, in commercial and investment real estate transactions, each side usually requires legal representation.

Do all attorneys have the qualifications and experience to service a commercial or investment real estate transaction?

> ### *Example:*
> **The Legal Adviser**
>
> Consider that you've just found your customer just what she asked for: class A office space; 3,000 square feet at $20 per square foot gross rent with a 10-year lease term. The lease is drafted by the landlord and sent to your customer for signature. Your customer takes the proposed lease to her attorney for review. Among the attorney's comments are the following: "You're paying too much money." "You're crazy for considering a lease of more than five years!"

Remember, the attorney also works for your customer and is trying to do the best job for the client. But, where is the deal going? Can you save it?

In commercial real estate, whether you are dealing with the owner/landlord, or buyer/tenant, ask who will be handling their legal representation when you take the listing or search assignment. Then ask whether their attorney specializes in commercial real estate. Often an owner will have an attorney who is a general practitioner but lacks experience in the complexities of commercial or investment transactions. At the time the listing is taken, you might recommend that your buyer seek out an attorney specializing in commercial real estate. If you don't have several specialists to recommend, suggest that your clients ask their local bar association, accountant, or banker for referrals.

Ask whether the owner has discussed the proposed sale or lease with an attorney and whether you might talk to the attorney. It would be wise to call the attorney and discuss your client's assignment; see whether the attorney thinks these actions are in the best interest of the client. Solve any differences of opinion before finalizing a transaction.

Attorneys are just one group of third-party advisers. Who else might be considered a third party advisor?

> ### *Example:*
> **The Accountant Advisor**
>
> Consider that a client is selling his building after 20 years of ownership. It takes you six months to locate a qualified buyer to make an offer that your client accepts.
>
> The owner now calls his accountant to advise him on what he is doing. The accountant tells the owner, "You can't sell the building; you will be killed with capital gains taxes!" Again, when taking the listing, ask the seller whether he has discussed the property with his accountant. There are alternatives to paying capital gains taxes. For example, the property can be leased, master-leased, or sold on a 1031 exchange basis, or taxes can be deferred through estate planning. You don't want to sell the building and then find that the owner's accountant opposes the sale. Talk to the accountant at the time of listing.

Buyers also have third-party advisers, such as mortgage brokers and bankers. All commercial customers should be prequalified. A good question might be "What price range do you feel comfortable with?" Be candid: "What is the maximum you are prepared to pay for a building?" Advise clients the price range of properties on the market; discuss typical commercial financing terms and expected down payments (in most cases 25 to 30 percent). Ask exactly how much money they have for a down payment. If they have not already done so, advise buyers to discuss the availability of financing with their banker. Buyers must realistically know what they can afford, and their financial advisor should be consulted before any property is looked at.

Because of the so-called mortgage meltdown of 2007 and 2008, there was a period during which borrowing money to purchase commercial properties was virtually impossible. Values of commercial properties declined in most areas of the country, often by 25 percent or more. Fortunately, a half-decade after the meltdown, the decline of commercial property values seems to have bottomed out.

Today many banks are again making commercial loans. The underwriting standards are stricter; but with good credit and a solid down payment (usually 25 to 30 percent), money is available. Also noteworthy, during this period of economic turmoil, credit unions started making more commercial loans and they continue to be active lenders today.

Special Financing Programs

When commercial transactions are being conducted, consider that special financing programs with lower down payment requirements or lower interest rates might be available. Inquire whether the customer plans to use any of the following agencies:

- Small Business Administration (SBA)
- Industrial Development Agency (IDA)
- Job Development Authority (JDA)

If so, recommend that the customer meet with program administrators before "shopping." Also bear in mind that these types of programs generally take longer to close than conventional financing, and this time element might affect the decision of a seller to accept such "subject to" offers. In other cases, these programs can help a business grow faster and can be successfully negotiated.

Most transactions will involve third-party advisers at some point. Generally, it is in the broker's best interest to recommend that clients and customers seek advice early in the transaction.

The Listing Information Checklist

Forms created for this book will assist in gathering the necessary information to list any type of commercial property. These forms are for information-gathering purposes only. A formal listing agreement is strongly recommended to properly list the property. Many REALTOR® organizations have standard listing forms available, or real estate brokers can seek assistance from an attorney.

Figure 1.4 depicts a sample Listing Information Checklist. This form will be used in conjunction with another standardized form for the specific type of building or land being listed. These forms will be reviewed in the chapters that follow.

Figure 1.4. | Listing Information Checklist

Location
1. Street address: _____
2. City: _____ State: _____ Zip: _____
3. Closest cross street: _____
4. County: _____ Section/Block/Lot: _____

Owner
5. Name or company: _____
6. Name of principal if company owned: _____
7. Owner's address: _____
8. City: _____ State: _____ Zip: _____
9. Phone: _____ Fax: _____ E-mail: _____
10. Web site: _____

Contact to Show
11. Name: _____
12. Phone: _____ Fax: _____ E-mail: _____

Owner's Attorney
13. Name: _____
14. Firm name: _____
15. Address: _____
16. City: _____ State: _____ Zip: _____
17. Phone: _____ Fax: _____ E-mail: _____

Property
18. Type: _____
19. For sale—price: _____ Price per square foot: _____
20. Real estate taxes: _____ Real estate taxes PSF: _____
21. Sales commission (%): _____
22. Lease commission rate and payment terms: _____

Note that the first section in the Listing Information Checklist provides details about the location (lines 1–4), the owner's information (lines 5–10), and a contact-to-show area (lines 11–12), all of which were discussed earlier in this chapter. The next section is for entering the owner's attorney contact information (lines 13–17). This is designed to prompt a discussion with the owner as the form is being completed. Question the attorney's commercial real estate experience and discuss any other appropriate advisers. The form then asks for general information about the property: type, price, and taxes (lines 18–20). Detailed information about the property, including lease information if appropriate, will be recorded on other forms that will be described in later chapters. The brokerage commission rates for sale and/or lease are then requested (lines 21–22); note that the compensation can also be a flat fee. This form, along with a detailed property sheet, will provide you with most of the information you need to know about the property.

Listing a property requires several types of documents. These include forms for gathering information about ownership, contacts, and the physical description of the property. Also necessary is a formal listing agreement between the broker and the owner or landlord that provides all the terms and conditions of the listing—including the amount of commission due, when it is earned, and when it is payable to the broker. In some cases, a separate commission agreement may be used.

■ Commercial Inventory

Today, the inventory of available commercial and investment properties is considerable. Locally, many REALTOR® organizations have multiple listing services and most list commercial properties as well as homes. The National Association of REALTORS® hosts a commercial Web site with many listings at *www.commercialsource.com*. Several national commercial property Web sites are searchable by state, county, or even town. Some of these sites provide free access, but many also have additional pay-for-service features; other sites charge membership fees. Many investors will buy property out of area or even out of state if the deal makes sense to them. A few examples of some of the larger Web sites are listed here:

- *www.loopnet.com*
- *www.propertyline.com*
- *www.commrex.com*
- *www.realup.com*
- *www.CoStar.com* (access restricted to the trade)
- *www.Showcase.com* (CoStar's public access site)

More information about these and other Web sites can be found in the appendix.

Review Questions

1. Commercial properties are owned by
   a. individuals.
   b. corporations.
   c. partnerships.
   d. any of these.

2. Who would be considered a third-party adviser?
   a. Real estate broker
   b. Attorney
   c. Engineer
   d. Title company

3. What is a typical down payment for a commercial property purchase?
   a. 50 percent
   b. 25–30 percent
   c. 10 percent
   d. 0 percent

4. When should a broker discuss third-party advisers with a property owner?
   a. At the time of a "meeting of the minds" of the parties
   b. After a contract or lease is drawn
   c. At the time a listing is taken
   d. Never

5. A property checklist is
   a. the only form you need to list commercial properties.
   b. part of a series of forms used to gather property information.
   c. the only agreement needed to list investment properties.
   d. a protection for your commission.

6. An exit strategy is of concern to
   a. mortgagors.
   b. user customers.
   c. investment clients.
   d. none of these.

7. Tenant representation agreements require a definition of
   a. the market area.
   b. the nature of the assignment.
   c. the client's obligations.
   d. all of these.

8. What is the main difference between residential and commercial customers?
   a. Value of purchase
   b. Repeat business
   c. Speed of closing
   d. Number of showings

9. The business cycle occurs
   a. every ten years.
   b. each year.
   c. every three to five years.
   d. none of these.

10. What types of properties may be investments?
    a. Industrial buildings
    b. Shopping centers
    c. Hotels
    d. All of these.

chapter two

All About Office Buildings

overview

Office buildings come in various shapes and sizes with different configurations and designs. Brokerage opportunities occur from selling such buildings, most often as investment properties but also in leasing space within buildings. This chapter will explore the physical attributes of office buildings and focus on the terms and clauses used when leasing space in buildings. ■

learning objectives

After completing this chapter, you will be able to

- identify the classification system used for office buildings,
- recognize what building features are important to office tenants,
- describe the concepts of square footage,
- describe the principles of investing in office buildings, and
- explain how to complete and use the office building checklist.

■ Key Terms

add-on factor
additional rent
as-builts
assumption agreement
common-area maintenance (CAM)

loss factor or core factor
net or usable square footage
rentable or gross or billable square footage
right of first refusal (ROFR)

tax escalation clause
tenant improvement allowance
triple net lease (NNN)
workletter

Classifications of Office Buildings

Office buildings are rated as Class A, Class B, or Class C spaces. The primary qualities of each type of building, and the reasons different types of commercial customers are attracted to these buildings, are described here.

Class A Office Buildings

"The best available space!"

- Attracts the highest-quality tenants
- Modern architecture
- Superior construction
- Excellent location
- Well-managed building
- Amenities/services

Class A office space is the best building available in the best location. It will be a relatively new building with modern architecture that projects an image of success for its tenants. There will usually be a large open entrance, often with an atrium. These building have many amenities. Inside you may find shops or restaurants, perhaps a health club, child care facility, or cafeteria. Security will be obvious, and the building will be immaculate.

Tenants in these buildings will be paying "top dollar" rents, the highest the market will bear. They are buying the prestigious image that the building projects. Tenants are making a statement to their customers: "Because we are the best, we can afford to be here!" They want to impress their clients.

What kinds of companies desire Class A space? These are companies whose customers come to their offices—law firms, Fortune 500 companies, corporate offices of banks and insurance companies, stock brokerage firms, and large ad agencies.

Class B Office Building

"A tired Class A!"

- Newer Class A building available
- Excellent building but no longer the best available space
- Captures the not-quite-A tenants
- Less-modern architecture

Time brings changes to every market. What was once "the" building—the finest, best building in which to locate—has now been replaced, only because a newer, more modern building has been built in the area. This new building is now the place to be. Every Class A building eventually becomes a victim of time, as the new place to be emerges. The former Class A is now a Class B. Class B buildings are still excellent, but they appeal to a different type of tenant. Depending on the general growth of an area, a building may change from an A to a B within five or ten years.

Class B space will also be expensive, but it will cost less than Class A and the cost tends to stabilize. The types of tenant who desires Class B space include companies that desire a "showplace" but that may not be quite as prestigious as those who seek Class A. Usually, Class B buildings also appeal to certain medical businesses. In Class B buildings, customers also commonly come to the tenant.

Medical office space. When considering medical businesses that may want to locate in a Class B office buildings, it is important to understand the unique requirements of a typical doctor's office. Generally, doctors' offices have multiple relatively small examining rooms, each with a sink. Such extensive plumbing usually requires that a building be constructed specifically for medical use. However, some medical businesses have less demand for plumbing, such as psychiatrists or optometrists. As a building progresses to Class B, the owner might consider modifying the space for medical use (especially on the ground floor or other lower level with easy access to plumbing), if the lease would be long enough to warrant the expense.

Class C Office Building

"Low-rent space"

- Older building
- Secondary-market tenants
- Approaching economic obsolescence
- Lacks image
- Secondary location

Class C buildings consist of two types: older buildings and buildings constructed to be highly functional. Some of these buildings may have been constructed 50 to 70 years ago. They might be in poor condition or be architecturally beautiful. However, because of their age, they may not have features that today's tenants expect. For example, the building might be a walk-up and have no elevators. There may be no central air-conditioning. The location might be poor and the number of bathrooms may be inadequate. The building might lack handicap access. Class C buildings might be found in what are now considered secondary locations—older or downtown areas away from newer office complexes.

Some newer buildings are purposely built as Class C buildings. They are designed to be highly functional, yielding the maximum percentage of usable office space. Built to current codes, they provide elevators and comply with the American with Disabilities Act. Although these buildings look functional, they might lack image or any architectural statement. You will not find any amenities in these buildings. Class C buildings rent for considerably less than the other classes.

Class C buildings serve the needs of commercial tenants who do not require an image. As a rule, these businesses do not have customers coming to their offices. Examples include back-office operations, bank processing centers, telemarketing companies, and sales offices. Class C tenants are predominately concerned with inexpensive rent; location is not a prime concern.

By understanding the different classes of office buildings, a licensee can properly direct leasing customers to buildings appropriate for their businesses.

Office Building Considerations

Phones and Computers

Today's office building buyers and tenants are very aware of technology; they want "smart" buildings. Such building must have adequate phone service and computer lines. When listing office buildings or the space within them, itemize what exists in the building, as well as what services in the area are available to the building. A technology list might include cable lines, digital satellite service, fiber optics, ISDN, or T1 lines.

Treatment of Utilities

Utilities include electricity, gas, oil (heat), and water. What is being included in the tenant's leases (paid by the landlord), and what is paid by the tenants? These items must be discussed and clarified in the lease.

In many small and in some large office buildings, each tenant has a separate meter for electric service and pays the provider directly for the metered service. In most large office buildings, landlords pay the utility provider for service to the entire building. In such cases, a utility charge is added to the tenants rent. For example, the rent might be $20 per square foot, and the tenant pays an additional charge of $2.25 per square foot for electricity.

Hours Open

Not all buildings are accessible 24 hours a day, seven days a week. But in today's era of international business and a 24/7 digital world, certain customers require round-the-clock access to their offices. This topic requires discussion when listing office space.

Ancillary Services

Learning what services are in a building and listing them for the potential tenant can be a good selling point in convincing someone to lease space in the building. Important services might include on-site cafeteria, health club/gym, and child care facilities. Other services may include various vending machines and overnight carrier drop boxes. From a buyer's point of view, some of these services represent additional sources of income for the building.

Parking

The customers of many tenants, especially those in Class A and Class B buildings, visit the offices. Can they easily find a parking space? Typical zoning regulations for office buildings specify four or five cars per 1,000 square feet of space. Such specifications may for provide adequate parking, but certainly more is better. In large buildings, people need to consider how far away from the building they will have to park and walk.

Consideration must be given to how many parking spaces are assigned to each tenant for their employees (and where those are located), the visitor parking for the tenant's customers, and the overall number of parking spaces serving the building. Is there security for the parking areas? Interior parking, underground parking, and tiered parking garages can increase the value of the building to both tenants and potential buyers.

Measuring Space

How much space do tenants get to use or occupy, and is it always the same amount of space that they have to pay for? Space is measured in square footage. Then the rent is calculated either on an annual or a monthly basis, depending on the market. In the Northeast, the rental cost is generally quoted as the annual cost per square foot. In some parts of the country, it is quoted as a monthly cost per square foot.

If the building has a single tenant (in any size building), that tenant uses all the space—"what you see is what you get." This means that if the unit is 1,000 square feet, the tenant's rent is calculated on 1,000 square feet.

Many buildings, however, are large and have multiple tenants. Landlords desire to be paid for every square inch of their building. In these properties, tenants exclusively occupy and use a certain amount of space, but they also share common areas with all the other tenants in the building. Thus, a tenant occupies **net or usable square footage**, paying for this space, as well as a proportionate share of the common area, known as the **rentable or gross or billable square footage**. Different terms for this concept are used in different areas and by various landlords. But this is an important concept in commercial real estate: Tenants often have to pay for more space than what they actually occupy.

How is space measured? The general authority on space measurement is BOMA, the Building Owners and Managers Association. Generally, a building is viewed in three ways. Certain parts of the building are considered structural and included in the base rental charge (e.g., thickness of exterior walls, exterior balconies, mechanical penthouse, upper stories of atriums, and major vertical penetrations).

The tenant-occupied unit square footage is measured from the inside of the walls within the unit and includes all usable space and storage areas. If there are demising walls (internal walls that divide or partition the space, like a private office) that space is included. Tenants must absorb HVAC convectors, columns, and interior building projections in their measurements.

Common areas of a building might consist of lobbies and atriums (at floor level), public corridors (and include the thickness of the corridor walls), elevators, staircases, public restrooms, janitorial, electric and phone closets, mechanical rooms, and loading docks. Such measurements will include the common areas on all floors.

When a building is constructed, an architect or an engineer will measure all the space in the building and determine the overall amount of usable square footage and the amount of common-area square footage. The percentage difference between the usable and rentable space is known as the **loss factor or core factor**. For example, a building is 100,000 square feet in total space; 15,000 square feet of that space is common area. The loss or core factor is 15 percent.

Landlords are entitled to get paid for all the space in their buildings, including the common areas. Two different methods are used to do this calculation; the add-on factor and the loss or core factor method.

Example:

Calculating Add-On Factor

The **add-on factor** is generally used in areas with high vacancy and low absorption rates. It is best illustrated by example. A tenant can use and occupy 10,000 square feet in a building. The landlord uses an add-on factor of 15 percent representing the common area of the building. For how much space is the tenant billed?

To calculate, consider the usable square footage occupied by the tenant to be 100 percent of the tenant's space and add 15 percent to that. The percentages are converted to decimals and multiplied by the usable amount of space.

$$100\% + 15\% = 115\% \text{ or } 1.15$$

$$10,000 \text{ SF} \times 1.15 = 11,500 \text{ SF}$$

The tenant must pay for 11,500 square feet of space.

Example:

Calculating Rentable Square Footage

The Loss Factor or Core Factor method of calculating **rentable square footage**, also known as **gross square footage or billable square footage**. This system of calculation is used in areas of generally low vacancy and relatively high absorption rates. In this method, the landlord provides the net or usable square footage and the loss or core factor percentage. The rentable square footage is then calculated according to this formula:

$$\frac{\text{Net square footage}}{1 - \text{Loss factor percentage}} = \text{Rentable square footage}$$

To determine the denominator for this equation, subtract from the whole number *1* (one) the loss factor percentage as a decimal. This provides the inverse of the loss factor.

For example, the landlord advises that the usable square footage is 1,000 square feet and the building has a 20 percent loss factor.

Step 1: Calculate the inverse of the loss factor (denominator for the equation).

$$20\% = 0.20$$

$$1 - 0.20 = 0.8$$

Step 2: Calculate the rentable square footage using the formula.

$$\frac{1,000 \text{ net SF}}{0.8} = 1,250 \text{ rentable SF}$$

Note, in contrast, that if the add-on formula were used for this calculation, the result would be as follows:

$$1,200 \text{ SF}$$

$$100\% + 20\% = 120\% \text{ or } 1.20$$

$$1,000 \text{ SF} \times 1.20 = 1,200 \text{ SF}$$

The result of using the loss factor or core factor method is that more money goes to the landlord.

Floor Plans

When listing space, consider that potential occupiers will need to know the dimensions of the unit or area so they can plan the location of offices, personnel, and office equipment. A complete listing requires a floor plan of the space or building.

As-Built

Sometimes, a new occupant can utilize the previous occupant's space as it has been built. **As-builts** show existing offices, walls, corridors, etc., within the subject space as they presently exist. A floor plan showing as-builts should also be obtained at the time of listing the space or building.

Tenant Improvements

As leases are negotiated, tenants may request that certain work be done in the desired space. This work might include dividing the space with walls or constructing individual offices. The requested work is usually described in a **workletter**. Who pays for the work, or buildout as it is also known, is a negotiable item between landlord and tenant.

Sometimes, in large office buildings, the owner sets a workletter amount when placing the available space on the market; this is known as a **tenant improvement allowance**. For example, the rent will be $28 per square foot and this amount includes a tenant improvement allowance of $5 per square foot. Here, the landlord will pay for the interior construction of the tenant's space up to a total cost of $5 per square foot. In this example, if the tenant were occupying 5,000 square feet, the landlord would contribute $25,000 toward the tenant's buildout. Any additional expense above that amount would be paid by the tenant. When listing large office buildings, always ask what the tenant improvement allowance is.

Lease Clauses

A lease may be defined as an agreement (actually a contract) whereby the owner (landlord) of real property gives the right of possession to another party (tenant) for a specific period of time (term of the lease) and for a specified consideration (rent).

In practical terms, the lease defines the following in a landlord/tenant relationship:

- Who does what?
- Who is responsible for what?
- Who pays, how much, and when?

The answers to these questions cover everything in the relationship, starting with a definition of the area/space to be rented, the length of time it will be rented, the rent to be paid, increases in rent, and additional rental charges for other items or services.

The subjects of tenant improvements, rent concessions, amounts of insurance, who pays for insurance, repair responsibilities, and other lease terms should all be clearly defined. Many legal clauses are necessary, including contingencies for default of the lease, procedures for catastrophes (i.e., a fire), subleasing or assigning the lease, and many others. Leases can be short standard forms or voluminous documents.

Note: It is an attorney's job, not a broker's, to prepare leases.

Common-Area Maintenance

A landlord of a shopping center, strip center, office or other type of property may provide common services to all the tenants in the building or center.

Examples of **common-area maintenance (CAM)** are:

- Cleaning
    - Exterior—parking lot
    - Interior—hallways, lobbies, rest rooms
    - Interior—office buildings: full service
- Lighting—signs, parking lot
- Landscaping
- Snow removal
- Rubbish removal
- Security
- Window washing
- Supplies—light bulbs, paper towels, etc.

The landlord's total cost of providing all these services is divided by the total square footage of the rentable area of the entire property; the result is the per-square-foot CAM charge. This amount is then proportionately charged to all the tenants, based on the square footage they occupy. CAM charges will vary according to the services provided, the size of the property, and geographic location. Common-area maintenance (CAM) expenses to the tenant are typically in the $2 to $4 per square foot range.

Example:
Calculating CAM

Mr. Jones rents a 2,000-square-foot store in a ten-store strip center that is 20,000 square feet in total size. The landlord provides common services to all the tenants, which total $60,000 per year in expense. How much will Jones pay in CAM charges for his store?

The CAM charges are calculated by dividing the total CAM expenses, $60,000, by the total square footage of the center, 20,000 square feet. This results in a CAM charge to be passed through to the tenants of $3 per square foot. Because Jones rents 2,000 square feet, his annual CAM charges will be $6,000 (2,000 SF × $3.00 PSF). This is considered **additional rent** and is usually billed monthly.

Gross Leasable Area

Gross leasable area (GLA) is the total square footage available for lease in a shopping center, office complex, or other type of building. The phrase is most commonly used to describe the size of large shopping centers and reflects the combined total square footage of all buildings and/or rentable floors in malls within the center.

Tax Escalation Clause

The **tax escalation clause** is also known as the tax stop or RET over base (real estate taxes divided by base). Many leases contain a tax escalation clause, which means that any increases in property taxes are proportionately passed to the tenants. The base taxes are the actual real estate taxes proportionate to the rental unit at the time of lease signing. Base taxes are paid by the landlord. RET over base reflect tax increases that would be paid by tenants. This clause will be found in most commercial leases, including retail, office, and industrial properties.

> ### *Example:*
> **Calculating Tax Escalation**
>
> A tenant occupies a 2,000-square-foot store in a shopping center with a gross leasable area (GLA) of 100,000 square feet and has a tax escalation clause in her lease. On the date the lease was signed, total real estate taxes on the shopping center were $400,000. The tenant occupies 2 percent of the shopping center (2,000 square feet in a 100,000-square-foot center). The landlord pays the base taxes. If the taxes increase after the lease commences, the tenant is responsible for paying her proportionate share of the increase.
>
> Two years later, real estate taxes increase by 3 percent. Under the tax escalation clause, the tenant must pay a proportionate share of the increase, which is calculated as follows:
>
> | | |
> |---|---|
> | Old shopping center real estate taxes | $400,000 |
> | Tax increase, 3% | + 12,000 |
> | Tenant's proportionate share of the tax increase, 2% | $240 |
>
> The tenant must now pay additional rent each year, reflecting the additional taxes of $240.

The increase in the example does not seem like a lot of money, but consider that this shopping center might have 30 to 40 tenants, each of whom signed leases with tax escalation clauses. Many of these tenants may be paying tax increases for many years. Say a tenant signed a ten-year lease—how many times will real estate taxes go up during that ten-year period?

When large shopping centers or office buildings have many tenants and varied leases, this additional rent can be significant and must be included when an investor projects income.

Option to Buy

Some leases offer tenants the opportunity to buy the property in the future. These leases should state a sales price or a method for determining the sales price at the time of purchase. A time limit in which to exercise this option to buy may also be included.

Assignment of Lease

Leases may or may not give the tenant the right to assign the lease to another party. Often, the landlord's approval is required. This clause can permit tenants to sell their leasehold interest in the property.

Assumption Agreement

An **assumption agreement** is an extremely important clause to the real estate broker. It covers after-lease events that pertaining to future commissions owed. These events may be a result of options to renew or extend leases, other options to buy, or the sale of leasehold interest.

The assumption agreement is effective in the event of a sale or an exchange of the property or the assignment of lease by the owner. At that time, the broker may be entitled to a future commission. The clause requires a document to be signed by buyers or assignees stating they will pay the broker all commissions payable under the lease(s). Without an assumption agreement, upon the sale of the building or assignment of lease, a broker has no commission claim against the new owner.

NNN Lease

A **triple net lease (NNN)** means that tenants pay all the expenses for a building. These expenses include utilities, taxes, and all repairs and maintenance. The landlord collects rent and has no expenses for the property.

Right of First Refusal (ROFR) Clause

Tenants who think they might wish to buy the building or property in the future may negotiate to have a **right of first refusal (ROFR)** clause included in the lease. What the clause says, in essence, is that if the owner decides to sell the property and obtains an offer to purchase that property, the tenant has the right to exactly match that offer in dollars and terms. If the tenant matches the offer, the owner must sell the property to that tenant.

It might happen that after a property is sold, you learn that one of the tenants has a right of first refusal clause in the lease and decides to buy the building. You might lose a commission and your buyer customer. Therefore, it is important to determine at the time of listing an office building for sale whether any tenants have a right of first refusal in their leases. If so, be sure your listing agreement states that if a sale to a tenant with a right of first refusal occurs as a result of an offer made by your customer, you are entitled to a sale commission. Be sure to disclose to any buyer to whom you show the building that a tenant has a right of first refusal.

■ Office Buildings as Investments

Rent Roll

A building's rent roll shows the projected rental income for all the available space in the building, whether or not the space is occupied. The two major categories of rental income are base rent and additional rent. The landlord may charge additional rent for items such as CAM (common-area maintenance), tax escalations, utilities, or insurance. This is called passing through expenses to the tenant. The rent roll is usually calculated on a per-square-foot basis, based on the space occupied.

Lease Escalations

The rent tenants pay usually increases over the term of the lease. These lease escalations can appear in many different forms, such as a fixed dollar amount, a fixed or variable percentage of increase, or an amount based on an index such as the Consumer Price Index. Escalations compound each year and are applied to the prior year's rent.

Lease Expirations

It is important to note when leases expire if they have any options for renewal. Buyers considering the purchase of office buildings as investments will look at these items, often over a multiyear period. They will then make adjustments for vacancy contingency, evaluate the expenses of the building, and develop a net operating income (NOI), which can be used to calculate value. This will be further discussed in the course, after we have examined other types of commercial properties because these investment concepts can be applied to most buildings.

■ Office Building Checklist

The Office Building Checklist, shown in Figure 2.1, will assist in listing office buildings or the space within them. This form focuses on the physical qualities of the building and/or rental unit. The financial analysis discussed in Chapter 3 is required to determine the value of the property. The Listing Information Checklist from Chapter 1 should be used for all property listings because it will help in obtaining ownership information and communication contacts. All the checklists in this book should be used in conjunction with formal listing agreements.

The left side of the Office Building Checklist form is for indicating information about the building in general. Even if you are only listing a part or a unit within the building, customers will be interested in the overall size and features of the entire building. On the right side of the form is the information about the specific rental unit.

Note that the area asking for rent information starts with the base rent per square foot. Then it has lines to add any additional rent and, finally, a line for total rent per square foot. Not all customers speak real estate language. Many prospective tenants can only relate to how much the space is going to cost them per month. To accurately calculate this cost for clients, use the total rent per square foot (including the base rent and additional charges imposed by the landlord). Multiply the total rent per square foot by the rentable (gross) square footage to determine the rent per month. Talk to customers in terms of how much the space will cost them per month.

In the comments section, note signage, if available, on directory or outside pylons. On smaller buildings, tenants may desire operable windows. Medical uses require extensive buildouts and plumbing. Some landlords welcome these tenants; others do not. Determine the owner's preference. Anything else unique about the building should be included in the comments (e.g., indoor parking).

Figure 2.1 | Office Building Checklist

Building Qualities

1. Class: _____
2. Total size (SF): _____
3. Site size: _____
4. # floors: _____
5. Year built: _____
6. Construction: _____
7. Elevator (Y/N): _____
8. Days/hours open: _____
9. Security (Y/N): _____
10. Parking: Total # spaces: _____
11. Parking: # visitor spaces: _____
12. Loss factor (%): _____
13. Technical services: _____
14. On-site ancillary services: (check box)
    ☐ Cleaning service provided by landlord
    ☐ Restaurant
    ☐ Cafeteria, full
    ☐ Cafeteria, vending machines
    ☐ Health club/gym
    ☐ Child care

15. Unit #: _____
16. Unit size: _____
17. Net (usable) SF: _____
18. Rentable (billable) SF: _____
19. Rent PSF: _____

Additional Rent

20. Utilities PSF: _____
21. CAM per SF: _____
22. Total rent per SF: _____
23. Rent per month: _____
24. Cleaning included (Y/N): _____
25. Tax escalation (Y/N): _____
26. Separate electric meter (Y/N): _____
27. NNN lease (Y/N): _____
28. ROFR (Y/N): _____
29. Lease term: _____
30. Annual escalations: _____
31. Tenant improvement
    Allowance: _____
32. # Assigned parking: _____

Unit Description

33. Comments: _____
_____
_____
_____
_____
_____
_____
_____

34. Attachments: ☐ Survey   ☐ Floor plans   ☐ As-builts

For building sale: Attach financial analysis

case study | Using the Office Building Checklist

Your client owns a 30,000-square-foot Class A office building. He asks you to lease a second-floor suite in his building. You meet to inspect the space and take the listing information. At the interview, you use the Listing Information Checklist (Figure 1.4) and Office Building Checklist (Figure 2.1) to gather the data you need. A completed Office Building Checklist is illustrated in Figure 2.2.

Figure 2.2 | Office Building Checklist (completed)

Building Qualities
1. Class: __A__
2. Total size (SF): __30,000__
3. Site size: __2.5 acres__
4. # floors: __3__
5. Year built: __1997__
6. Construction: __Joisted Masonry__
7. Elevator (Y/N): __Y__
8. Days/hours open: __24/7__
9. Security (Y/N): __Y__
10. Parking: Total # spaces: __175__
11. Parking: # visitor spaces: __25__
12. Loss factor (%): __15%__
13. Technical services: __Fiber optic and cable__
14. On-site ancillary services: (check box)
    - ☐ Cleaning service provided by landlord
    - ☐ Restaurant
    - ☐ Cafeteria, full
    - ☐ Cafeteria, vending machines
    - ☐ Health club/gym
    - ☐ Child care

15. Unit #: __4__
16. Unit size: __5,000 SF__
17. Net (usable) SF: __5,000 SF__
18. Rentable (billable) SF: __5,750 SF__
19. Rent per SF: __$20.00__

Additional Rent
20. Utilities PSF: __2.25__
21. CAM per SF: __2.75__
22. Total rent per SF: __$25.00__
23. Rent per month: __$11,979__
24. Cleaning included (Y/N): __N__
25. Tax escalation (Y/N): __Y__
26. Separate electric meter (Y/N): __N__
27. NNN lease (Y/N): __N__
28. ROFR (Y/N): __N__
29. Lease term: __5 years__
30. Annual escalations: __4%__
31. Tenant improvement
    Allowance: __$5 PSF__
32. # Assigned parking: __20__

Unit Description

33. Comments:
    __2nd floor unit—signage in directory__
    _____
    _____
    _____
    _____
    _____
    _____

34. Attachments: ☐ Survey   ☐ Floor plans   ☐ As-builts

For building sale: Attach financial analysis

Figure 2.3 | Calculation of Total Rent per Square Foot

Base rent per SF	$20.00
Additional rent	
Utilities (electric) per SF	2.25
Common-area maintenance (CAM) charges	2.75
Total rent per SF	$25.00

When interviewing the building owner, you learn that he'd like to lease a second-floor suite of 5,000 square feet. The clients will want to know about the building in general, and the information you gather on the left side of the form will allow you to give them a good description. On the right side of the form, you detail the information about the available unit. Of particular importance are lines 17 through 23. The net usable space—that which the client can actually occupy—is 5,000 square feet, as listed on line 17. The common area for the building is 15 percent (line 12), which allows you to calculate the gross (billable) square footage (line 18) by multiplying (using the Add-On factor) the net square footage by 115 percent (5,000 × 1.15 = 5,750), yielding 5,750 as the gross square footage.

The base rent for the space is $20 per square foot (line 19). In addition, the tenants are required to pay additional rent for electricity, which is entered on line 20 under utilities and common-area maintenance (CAM) charges, which are entered on line 21. To calculate the tenant's total cost of occupying the space, the total rent per square foot must be calculated (*see* Figure 2.3).

Many tenants have difficulty relating to square footage and per-square-foot costs. They relate better if the rent expenses are quoted as the total cost per month, which in Figure 2.2 was calculated and inserted on line 23 (*see* Figure 2.4).

Based on these figures, from a marketing point of view, one might quote the rent to a potential tenant as "the rent for the 5,000-square-foot unit, including common area, electricity, and CAM charges, will cost a total of $12,000 per month."

The rest of the lease terms discussed in this chapter, and those desired by the owner in this example, have been entered on the sample form.

Figure 2.4 | Calculation of Rent per Month

The rentable (billable) square feet multiplied by the total per square foot equals the annual rent, which is divided by 12 (months) to determine the rent per month.	
This example:	
Rentable (billable) SF (line 18)	5,750
Multiplied by total rent per SF (line 22)	× $25
Annual rent	$143,750
Divided by 12 (number of months)	÷ 12
Yields rent per month (line 23)	$ 11,979

Review Questions

1. The phrase *best available space* describes what type of building?
   a. Level 1
   b. Superior
   c. Class A
   d. Grade A

2. What is the primary factor that changes the classification of an office building?
   a. Competition
   b. Time
   c. Improvements
   d. Transportation

3. Tenants who rarely have clients visit them may be interested in what type of building?
   a. Function Level D
   b. Type 4
   c. Class C
   d. Class B

4. A "smart" building might have what services?
   a. T1–T3 lines
   b. Fiber optics
   c. Cable lines
   d. All of these

5. Rentable square footage is the amount of space
   a. billed to the client.
   b. occupied by the client.
   c. in the entire building.
   d. represented by the broker.

6. A loss factor
   a. decreases the cost to rent.
   b. increases the cost to rent.
   c. does not affect the cost to rent.
   d. refers to vacancies.

7. What is it called when a landlord allocates money to build out a new tenant's space?
   a. Workletter
   b. Improvement credit
   c. Tenant improvement allowance
   d. Building renovation fund

8. A right of first refusal
   a. permits an existing tenant to buy the building.
   b. can cost a broker the commission.
   c. can cause an offer to be rejected.
   d. all of these.

9. What is used to calculate the cost of space per month?
   a. Net square footage and base rent
   b. Gross square footage and base rent
   c. Net square footage and total rent per square foot
   d. Rentable square footage and total rent per square foot

10. In a triple net lease (NNN), the landlord pays
    a. real estate taxes.
    b. for structural repairs only.
    c. building insurance.
    d. none of these.

chapter three

Retail Properties

overview

Shopping is done in small stores on Main Street or in giant regional malls containing 40, 50, 60, or more stores. Local strip centers and convenience stores can service a neighborhood's daily needs. Traditional supermarkets, outlet centers, power centers, and malls all sell to retail consumers. In this chapter, we will examine the different types of buildings used for retail sales, the considerations of retailers in finding sites, and some of the terms used in this industry. ∎

learning objectives

After completing this chapter, you will be able to

- define retail characteristics and terms,
- describe the concept of plain vanilla shell,
- identify how specialty retail businesses are sold, and
- describe the tools used by retailers to evaluate locations.

■ Key Terms

anchor tenant	end cap	plain vanilla shell
demographics	percentage lease	tenant mix

Retail Buildings

A store can be freestanding or attached to other stores or structures. A store can be small, a few hundred or thousand square feet, or it might be a huge building of over 100,000 square feet.

Strip center is a term used for a single building that has been divided into five to ten stores. A neighborhood center may be somewhat larger with several attached or closely grouped buildings, which might be divided into multiple stores.

Shopping centers generally have a large (10,000 square feet or more) anchor store, attached to an expanded strip center with perhaps 10 to 15 stores, or more. An anchor store in this size range might be a national drug store chain or a considerably larger store, such as a supermarket or department store. These stores have national or regional name recognition. They do their own advertising, which draws people to their store and consequently to the other stores located next to them. This reduces the need for other stores in that center to advertise. Anchor tenants are found in neighborhood centers or shopping centers.

From the landlord's perspective, the anchor tenant will draw other tenants to the center and reduce the possibility of vacant stores. Traditionally, anchor tenants are charged rents below market value, but they will pay their proportionate share of all expenses of the property. However, the other tenants, who reap the rewards of the anchor store's advertising and national appeal, typically pay a higher-than-market rent.

Next in size are regional shopping centers, which may have several anchor-quality tenants and many small stores. Malls are even larger in scope and are often enclosed. Generally, large shopping centers, regional centers, and malls will have on-site management and leasing agents. Brokers in the area may work with them to place tenants in available space.

Outlet centers have become very popular. All the tenants in the outlet center are restricted to major name retailers and manufacturers selling at discount. Often, the merchandise sold in these stores is considered seconds or irregulars or are from discontinued lines.

Pad sites or out parcels are areas of land, usually found in front of or on the outskirts of a shopping center or larger retail complex. These might be at the entrance to the center but are usually away from the main shopping area. This land may be leased or sold to a company that builds its own facility. These sites are commonly used for fast food establishments or restaurant/bar operations.

Anchor Tenants

Most large shopping centers have an **anchor tenant** that usually occupies the largest store in that center. This household-name store (often a supermarket, department store, or national retail chain) draws people to the store and, consequently, to the shopping center. The anchor store usually does extensive advertising, which effectively benefits all the tenants of the center. The surrounding or attached stores gain free exposure to the people coming to shop at the anchor store.

In order to attract an anchor tenant with reduced rent, owners will likely write a triple net lease (NNN). In this manner, the anchor tenant will pay a proportionate share of the full property taxes and common-area maintenance charges and be responsible for the repairs and maintenance of its own building. Often, the anchor tenant will occupy half or more of the shopping center's overall square footage, so these additional lease charges are important to an investor's bottom line.

Because of the draw of this lead store to the center, other businesses will want to be in the shopping center. They will have the advantage of the "free" advertising generated for the center by the anchor tenant. The shopping center owner can now charge these smaller tenants much higher rents. The owner's profit, in other words, will come from these smaller tenants.

In many areas, traditional shopping centers have been replaced by power centers and mega-malls. Power centers take on the unique appearance of a cluster of big-box retailers and usually consist of four to five very large anchor-quality tenants on the same property, with little or no small stores on site. In these cases, the concepts remain the same, but the anchor stores may also be paying substantial rents. The marketing strategy for power centers is that several anchors will draw even more people to the shopping area.

■ Other Retail Terms

End Cap

Visualize a five-store strip center, with one building divided into five retail spaces. The interior stores are called in-line stores. They share common walls on both sides with adjacent stores. On each end of the center are stores called **end caps**. The businesses in the center might display a sign on the front of their individual store, but only the end-cap tenants can display a second sign on the side of the building. This additional visibility makes the end-cap space more valuable than an in-line store space. It is also possible for end caps to provide drive-through windows. This feature is usually important to banks and fast-food restaurants.

Tenant Mix

When listing stores for lease in a retail center, note the other tenancies located in that center. This is called the **tenant mix**. For example, two pizza parlors would not be located in the same strip center. But it is equally important to note the types of stores located in the immediate area of the property. You would not solicit a video store if one was already located two blocks away.

AM Side

Certain businesses will desire to be located on the AM or PM side of the road. Generally, traffic will be heavier in one direction of a roadway in the morning as people go to work and heavier in the other direction in the afternoon as the same folks return home from their jobs.

Coffee shops and doughnut stores are good examples of companies that would want to locate on the AM side of the road. Returning home, someone may want to stop at convenience store to pick up milk. Liquor stores and video stores also prefer a PM side.

Far Corner

When you stop at a traffic light, you look across the intersection at a store on the far corner. Spontaneously, you decide you need to buy something there; you can easily turn into the site after you cross the intersection. The far corner concept is to capitalize on those stopped at the light. They are "forced" to look at building signs and other advertising that entice them to pull in and make a purchase. Pulling in is easy because customers have time to make the decision and they have not yet passed the store. Many drug stores and convenience stores prefer far corners.

Plain Vanilla Shell

Ever notice how the interior of every store in certain retail chains is the same? These chains desire a specific finish for their stores so that no matter in what location customers find themselves, the products will all be in the same aisle.

There are two categories of construction: raw building and finishing work. Those tenants who want the same image for every store will often rent on the basis of a **plain vanilla shell** and do all the interior construction (finishing work) themselves.

The phrase *plain vanilla shell* is generally accepted to mean delivering the space ready for occupancy, with unpainted sheetrocked walls, flooring, lighting, electric outlets, and bathrooms installed. The tenant finished the interior. The plain vanilla shell concept requires a specific understanding between the parties about the work to be done by the landlord. In some cases, the building is delivered raw, with cinder-block walls, concrete floors, and electric and plumbing lines in place. The tenant must complete all remaining work. The rent, when leased on a plain-vanilla-shell basis, is considerably lower than if the landlord were required to finish the space.

Finishing Space

There are two extremes as to how space will be rented and delivered. "As is" condition means the tenant leases the space as it is, with any cleanup or construction to be completed by the tenant. The other model is for landlords and tenants to negotiate work or improvements to be done to the space. The specific projects to be done are listed in a workletter. Sometimes, these tenant improvements are paid for by the landlord, sometimes the tenant pays, and sometimes the expenses are shared.

■ Retail Specialty Businesses

Certain retail businesses have unique characteristics that create a value based more on the business itself than any real estate involved. The property may be sold; if a lease, the leasehold interest may be transferred with the sale of the business. The property or lease is valued separately and added to the cost of purchasing the business. Here are some examples of terms and concepts vital to retail specialty businesses.

Restaurants

A consideration in determining the market value of a restaurant business is the number of persons permitted to occupy the restaurant. This is expressed in terms of the number of seats.

The number of seats indicates the maximum number of meals that can be served and, consequently, the profit that might be generated.

Very often, the parking requirement, found in zoning codes for food use, may include one space for each table in the restaurant. A table might be defined as seating four patrons. A typical restaurant parking requirement is one car for each table, plus one car for every employee. Thus, the parking issue reflects on the permitted occupancy.

Restaurateurs tend to develop their establishment over a few years. If they then decide to sell, they value the business based on the number of weekly meals served, gross income, and the restaurant's reputation. This type of sale will include all the equipment and furnishings. In the commercial real estate world, it is known as selling the key or a turnkey sale.

Leases for restaurants are typically long, ten years or more, and are assignable. When the business is bought, this leasehold interest will be transferred or also sold. Without the lease protection, which allows the operation to be maintained for a significant period, the business has little or no value.

Cash Businesses

Certain businesses traditionally sell products that are mostly purchased with cash. Examples include stationery stores, delicatessens, hair salons, or convenience stores. The amount of business done weekly becomes the basis for the business value and sale price. Depending on the type of business, a multiple of the weekly sales report determines the asking price. For example a business may be worth 20 times its weekly sales.

To verify this representation, the buyer may work with the seller for a number of weeks (called an observation period) verifying each day's income.

Gas Stations

In the case of gas stations, one measure of value is the amount of gas sold each month (gallons pumped). A repair business or convenience store income may add additional value.

Consideration is also given to the gasoline company that is franchising the station and the length of that lease agreement. The location of gas stations is often on a high-traffic corner or road. The idea of highest and best use is to maximize the potential income from the site to the property owner. Redeveloping the gas station to a fast-food restaurant or bank facility may prove to be more profitable.

■ Site Considerations and Concerns

Retail Zoning

Today, professional services may also be located in retail sectors. It is not uncommon to find a dentist, a doctor, or an accountant's office in a retail center, but these businesses may be classified for office use in zoning regulations.

Consequently, there may be different parking requirements for different businesses. For example, a typical parking requirement for retail areas may be three cars for every 1,000 square feet of space, while office use might require four or five cars for every 1,000 square feet of space. These heightened parking requirements may not be available in many commercial areas, and an office tenant, therefore, could not be put into that space without a zoning variance.

Permitted Business Uses

Not every business use is permitted in every location. The local health department may limit the number of "wet" tenants that use an excessive amount of water in a strip or shopping center. Perhaps only one restaurant or food establishment will be permitted. Often, anchor tenants will have lease restrictions for the rest of the center. For example, a supermarket may not permit an additional butcher shop or a bakery to be located in the center.

Location

When considering retail space, potential buyers or tenants need to evaluate activity at the location for their particular product line or business. They will want to know about access, whether there is a traffic light, how much parking is available, etc.

They will also request traffic counts, which are available from most municipalities, or order their own traffic study. How many vehicles pass their store each day is an important consideration.

Demographics

How many potential customers are in an area to support a retail operation? This question is answered by **demographic** reports, which show population, median household income, breakdowns by age, number of houses owned versus rental units, and many other factors. These statistics are often listed by rings on a map showing figures within X miles of the site—for example, one-, three-, or five-mile circles around the site. When listing retail properties, ask owners whether they have traffic counts and other demographics available. Figure 3.1 is a summary chart representing a partial demographic report for a retail location in densely populated Long Island, New York. It indicates various statistics within a one-, three-, and five-mile radius of the site.

Many of the commercial listing services include access to demographic reports for the properties listed on them. The sample in Figure 3.1 was obtained from a property listed on Loopnet, Inc., which can be accessed at *www.loopnet.com*.

Private demographics providers offer various kinds of reports giving other types of information and more extensive statistical breakdowns.

■ Special Retail Lease

Many of the typical lease clauses, presented in the office building chapter, may also be applicable to retail leases. In addition, there is an item that pertains only to retail, a percentage lease, which could appear as a lease clause or an entirely separate lease document.

Figure 3.1 | Partial Demographic Report

Population	1-mi.	3-mi.	5-mi.
2011 Male Population	9,654	40,465	85,013
2011 Female Population	9,199	40,838	87,355
% 2011 Male Population	51.21%	49.77%	49.32%
% 2011 Female Population	48.79%	50.23%	50.68%
2011 Total Adult Population	14,398	63,324	133,261
2011 Total Daytime Population	20,701	83,336	207,653
2011 Total Daytime Work Population	12,447	48,743	131,346
2011 Median Age Total Population	34	38	40
2011 Median Age Adult Population	42	45	47
2011 Age 0–5	1,570	6,385	13,037
2011 Age 6–13	1,873	7,606	17,168
2011 Age 14–17	1,012	3,988	8,901
2011 Age 18–20	793	2,873	5,715
2011 Age 21–24	1,144	4,063	7,550
2011 Age 25–29	1,523	5,670	9,632
2011 Age 30–34	1,529	5,765	10,721
2011 Age 35–39	1,452	5,816	11,718
2011 Age 40–44	1,490	6,249	13,602
2011 Age 45–49	1,373	6,391	14,613
2011 Age 50–54	1,132	5,788	13,670
2011 Age 55–59	852	4,853	11,605
2011 Age 60–64	850	4,131	9,506
2011 Age 65–69	631	3,284	7,360
2011 Age 70–74	542	2,655	5,835
2011 Age 75–79	460	2,136	4,550
2011 Age 80–84	357	1,726	3,382
2011 Age 85+	271	1,924	3,801
% 2011 Age 0–5	8.33%	7.85%	7.56%
% 2011 Age 6–13	9.93%	9.36%	9.96%
% 2011 Age 14–17	5.37%	4.91%	5.16%
% 2011 Age 18–20	4.21%	3.53%	3.32%
% 2011 Age 21–24	6.07%	5.00%	4.38%
% 2011 Age 25–29	8.08%	6.97%	5.59%
% 2011 Age 30–34	8.11%	7.09%	6.22%
% 2011 Age 35–39	7.70%	7.15%	6.80%
% 2011 Age 40–44	7.90%	7.69%	7.89%
% 2011 Age 45–49	7.28%	7.86%	8.48%
% 2011 Age 50–54	6.00%	7.12%	7.93%
% 2011 Age 55–59	4.52%	5.97%	6.73%
% 2011 Age 60–64	4.51%	5.08%	5.52%
% 2011 Age 65–69	3.35%	4.04%	4.27%
% 2011 Age 70–74	2.87%	3.27%	3.39%
% 2011 Age 75–79	2.44%	2.63%	2.64%
% 2011 Age 80–84	1.89%	2.12%	1.96%
% 2011 Age 85+	1.44%	2.37%	2.21%

Source: Loopnet, Inc., *www.loopnet.com*

Percentage Leases

When a tenant signs a **percentage lease**, part of the rent paid to the landlord is a percentage of the sales of the retailer. The percentage may apply to all sales from the first day of the lease, but more commonly a breakeven point is established.

Retailers often look at their business year, anticipating all the expenses for the year, and consequently consider the year as starting without profit. However, the business reaches a point when the store starts to make a profit for the year. In a percentage lease, a breakeven or threshold dollar amount is determined and the percentage is negotiated. After sales reach the breakeven point, the tenant pays the agreed percentage of all sales thereafter as additional rent.

The breakeven point is a dollar amount of sales, after which the tenant must remit the percentage of sales to the landlord as additional rent. When creating a breakeven point, the following formula is used:

$$\frac{\text{Annual rent}}{\text{Percentage of sales}} = \text{Breakeven point}$$

Example:
Calculating a Breakeven Point

A tenant's base rent is $5,000 per month, or $60,000 a year. The tenant also agrees to a percentage lease and to pay 5 percent of sales after reaching a breakeven point.

$$\frac{\$60,000}{0.05} = \$1,250,000$$

Once store sales reach $1,250,000, the tenant will pay 5 percent of all future sales to the landlord in addition to the monthly base rent of $5,000.

■ Retail Building Checklist

This Retail Building Checklist (*see* Figure 3.2) follows the pattern of the other forms used in this course. The left side of the form primarily describes the building, which could vary from a small or large freestanding store to a strip center or regional mall. Of particular importance on this form are lines 12 and 13. In some areas, multiple retail zoning codes allow for different uses. For example, is professional use by a dentist or an accountant permitted under this zoning code? Clarify, if necessary, under the comments section. Are there any restrictions to the type of occupancy or time of use for the building or store?

A store being leased may be a freestanding building or located in a neighborhood center or an enclosed mall. Small stores might have a simple base rent per month or be located in an enclosed mall with gross and net size considerations and possible additional rent charges. The checklist provides lines for all these possibilities and other items unique to the retail properties discussed in this chapter.

Tenant mix, another important reminder in listing retail space for rent is indicated on line 32. This calls for noting other tenancies in the building or surrounding area on the back of the form.

Comments should include the owner's preference for delivery of space, "as is" versus "tenant improvements" and any other unique features of the property or surrounding area.

To have all the listing information one needs to list a retail property, a Listing Information Checklist (discussed in Chapter 1) should also be completed. For a sale of retail investment property, one would also need to complete Investment Properties: Financial Analysis Checklist (found in Chapter 5). In all cases, a separate formal listing agreement should also be obtained.

Figure 3.2 | Retail Building Checklist

Building qualities:
1. Type: _____
2. Total size (SF): _____
3. Site size: _____
4. Freestanding (Y/N): _____
5. # Floors: _____
6. Year built: _____
7. Construction: _____
8. Elevator (Y/N): _____
9. Days/hours Open: _____
10. Security (Y/N): _____

Parking:
11. Total # spaces: _____
12. Zoning: _____
13. Restricted uses: _____
_____

Store for lease:
14. End cap (Y/N): _____
15. Anchors (Who): _____

Store description:
16. Unit #: _____
17. Store size: _____
18. Net (usable) SF: _____
19. Rentable (billable) SF: _____
20. Rent per SF: _____

Additional rent:
21. Utilities per SF: _____
22. CAM per SF: _____
23. Total rent per SF: _____
24. Rent per month: _____
25. Separate electric meter (Y/N): _____
26. NNN lease (Y/N): _____
27. Tax escalation (Y/N): _____
28. Percentage lease (Y/N): _____
29. ROFR (Y/N): _____
30. Lease term: _____
31. Annual escalations: _____
32. Tenant mix: List other tenants in this building or surrounding area on the back of this page.

Comments:
_____
_____
_____
_____
_____
_____
_____

Attachments: ☐ Survey ☐ Floor plans ☐ As-builts
☐ Traffic counts ☐ Demographics

For building sale: Attach financial analysis

Review Questions

1. What type of store would be an anchor tenant?
   a. A store that sells marine supplies
   b. Department store
   c. Local restaurant
   d. Gas station

2. What is an advantage of renting an end cap?
   a. Additional signage
   b. Possible drive-through
   c. Greater visibility
   d. All of these

3. A doughnut shop might request what type of location?
   a. Far corner
   b. AM side of the road
   c. PM side of the road
   d. Near corner

4. If tenants desire to finish the interior construction of a store themselves, they request to lease space on what basis?
   a. Triple net
   b. Plain vanilla shell
   c. Percentage lease
   d. Tenant improvement allowance

5. Which of the following can affect the type of business that will rent a specific store?
   a. The highest and best use of the site
   b. Higher parking requirements for different uses
   c. Building condition
   d. None of these

6. What type of report provides population and medium household income information?
   a. Traffic counts
   b. Marketing analysis
   c. Demographics
   d. Neighborhood study

7. What alternative type of lease would be used only for retail tenants?
   a. NNN
   b. Gross
   c. Option
   d. Percentage

8. What is the main value of an anchor tenant to a landlord?
   a. Pays much higher rents
   b. Draws customers to the site
   c. Draws other tenants to the site
   d. Always has a percentage lease

9. A building divided into five to ten stores is known as a
   a. neighborhood center.
   b. strip center.
   c. shopping center.
   d. freestanding building.

10. When listing a retail store for rent, the agent should pay particular attention to the
    a. tenant mix.
    b. desired lease terms.
    c. existing buildout.
    d. signage.

Industrial Buildings and Their Physical Characteristics

overview

Industrial buildings are used to store and distribute goods and products. Pieces and parts of everything imaginable are created in factories and assembled in manufacturing plants. New ideas are cultivated in research and development (R&D) buildings. Clients interested in these types of buildings look for physical characteristics unique to these structures. With strong tenants, industrial buildings may also be good investment properties. ■

learning objectives

After completing this chapter, you will be able to

- define the terminology used by industrial clients,
- recognize the importance of site inspections,
- describe the basics of environmental inspections, and
- learn how to complete an Industrial Property Checklist.

■ Key Terms

ceiling height	environmental reports	overhead door
column spans	loading dock	tail-board

Site Inspections

In commercial real estate, much information about listings is shared by brokers with other brokers through distribution of flyers about the property. But, especially with industrial buildings, the best way to know a building is to conduct a physical inspection of that building. For example, you might receive a flyer for a 20,000-square-foot warehouse located on an acre of land. The flyer might even feature a picture of the building and other descriptive information. But it does not say where the building is located on the site. Why is that important?

Early in my own real estate career, I learned some things the hard way. I matched up a customer's request for a 20,000–square-foot warehouse with a flyer of a building I had never seen. When I took my customer to the site, he would not get out of my car to even look at the building. I asked him what was wrong. My customer looked at the building, which was located in the middle of the property, and advised me that the 55-foot tractor trailers trucks used in his business would not be able to maneuver around the building to the loading area. (If the building location abutted one side of the property, access would not have been a problem.)

Several lessons can be learned from this story. First, always inspect properties before presenting them to a customer. I also recommend visiting the customer's existing location. See for yourself how the business operates. Look at how supplies or goods are shipped to the business. How does the business distribute its products? You will find these visits extremely helpful in matching up a building to your customers' needs.

Size of Buildings and Sites

Listing industrial buildings requires both the size of the building and the size of the site on which it is located. A site plan is essential for showing where the building is constructed on the land. The number of parking spaces is important, as is the location of the parking areas on the site. Industrial buildings can have multiple floors, which are most likely be serviced by freight elevators. With these structures, consider the issue of floor load. How much weight (per square foot) can each floor support? The capacity of freight elevators is also measured by how much weight they can carry.

Truck Access

Discuss the size of trucks used by your customer and the size of trucks that deliver supplies or goods to your client. Evaluate buildings based on their location on a site. Note whether access roads to the site have any truck restrictions.

Over the past few years, the escalating cost of oil and diesel fuel has contributed to the increasing cost of shipping goods by truck. The value of warehouse buildings has a direct relationship to the building's proximity to major roadways. Access right off a major highway increases the value of that building; the greater the distance that truckers have to drive to get to a building, the less value it has. Repeated trips, even over relatively short distances, can add up to many miles over the years. Business owners who require trucking to move their products seek building locations that minimize the distance to major roadways.

Building Features

Columns Placements

Most industrial buildings have a roof that is supported by columns and girders. When I first started out in this business, I had a customer who asked me to find him a 25,000-square-foot warehouse for his carpet business. I took him to a building I had previously inspected that appeared to me to be a typical warehouse. Once inside, my customer told me the building would not work for him. He explained that he receives 30-foot rolls of carpets, which they then cut down and install in office buildings. This building had typical column placements, or **column spans**, which are usually spaced 20 to 25 feet apart. Consequently, the customer's goods could neither be moved around nor laid out to cut.

This customer required a warehouse with unusually wide column placement or no columns at all. When a building has no columns, it is usually referred to as having a clear span. Such buildings are available, but usually at a higher cost. The story reemphasizes the need to investigate what your customer's business is all about.

Another point about columns: Many businesses store their vehicles inside the building. This is typical of electric and plumbing contractors and phone and cable companies, especially if they are located in city areas with little or no outside storage or parking. When listing an industrial building, ask for a floor plan that shows the column placements.

Ceiling Height

Industrial buildings measure **ceiling height** from the floor to the bottom of the roof supports (the girders). This is called feet under steel. For example, the term *15 feet US* refers to *15 feet under steel*.

Industrial buildings, in particular warehouses and distribution centers, are used for the storage of goods or materials. Often, these items arrive on pallets, which are stacked atop each other to maximize space. In these buildings, the focus is on cubic volume more than square footage. The greater the height of a building, the greater the cubic capacity. The larger the capacity, the greater the building's value.

Numerous companies literally raise the roof of industrial buildings. Consider your clients' needs for more space. Perhaps they can buy a smaller building and raise the roof to have the capacity they require. This process is relatively inexpensive as compared to the cost per foot for a purchase. You may be able to service your customer better and save them a considerable amount of money.

Loading

When listing industrial buildings, you must indicate by count how many trucks can load or unload goods at the same time. A truck to access these buildings in three basic ways:

- **Overhead doors** are essentially giant garage doors of the type you might have at home, but these are large enough to allow trucks to actually drive into the building.
- **Loading docks** are raised platforms, usually outside of the building, that bring the bay of the truck body level with the floor of the building. In that manner, the goods can be easily rolled off the truck.

- **Tail-boards** serve a similar purpose but can take several forms depending on the location (height) of the building floor. In an elevated floor situation, you may see a garage door that appears to start about three feet off the ground. When the door is opened, the truck backs up to it and the goods are rolled off the truck. When the building floor is at ground level, the truck backs down a declining plane or ramp until the truck bay is even with the ground level of the building. This type of tail-board may be found outside the building or constructed in the building and used in conjunction with an overhead door. Tail-boards are also referred to as loading bays.

Floor Plans

Many industrial buildings are quite large and may be divided into different areas. These sections may not have been built at the same time and might also have different ceiling heights. It would be important in a listing to note that a 30,000-square-foot warehouse had 20,000 square feet of space with 22 feet US (under steel) and 10,000 square feet with 16 feet US. In a divided building, note on the floor plan the ceiling heights of the different areas. Also, be sure the column placements are noted in the floor plan.

Percentage of Office Space

Typically, industrial buildings have 10 percent of the space built for office use. One exception is research and development buildings, which are usually 50 percent office space. It is important to note this percentage when listing these types of buildings.

Technical Services

Industrial businesses can operate around the clock and provide services locally, regionally, nationally, or internationally. They have a need for the latest communication and computer equipment and lines. When listing these properties, note what technical services are in the building or available in that area. The existing occupant may not use the service, but the new buyer or tenant may require it. Note services such as cable lines, digital satellite, fiber optics, ISDN, or T1–T3 lines.

Heating, Ventilating, and Air Conditioning (HVAC)

All parts of industrial buildings may not have the same heating and air-conditioning servicing. In many cases, just the office areas are air conditioned. Heating and air-conditioning must be determined when listing the property. In addition, investigate the type of fuel used (gas, oil, other).

Electric Capacity

For the listing, determine the amperage to the building.

Sprinklers

Determine and note whether the building has sprinklers. The most common building sprinklers are called wet pipe. In these systems, water is constantly maintained within the sprinkler piping and released through the sprinkler heads in the event of a fire. Because wet pipes contain water, these areas of the building must remained heated in cold-weather environments. Another type of sprinkler is called dry pipe, which is filled with pressurized air or nitrogen instead of water. When these sprinklers are activated, the air escapes. Water then enters the pipes and discharges from the sprinkler heads.

Standpipe systems are found mostly in highrises and other large buildings. Standpipes are an internal system of water mains connected to hose stations, which are turned on in the event of a fire.

Refrigeration

Certain buildings have refrigeration and freezers. In such cases, determine the size, cubic capacity, and temperature ranges of such units.

Floor Drains

Buildings with refrigerators or freezers—or that once had such facilities—will usually have floor drains, as will many food and beverage manufacturing plants and other buildings where the businesses may have to clean or wash down machinery. Floor drains are sometimes misused for disposal of chemicals and other waste, or they may have been used improperly by a previous owner or tenant.

Floor drains will therefore raise a red flag to prospective buyers and new tenants, who will want to be assured that the building has no environmental problems. It is recommended that when listing a building with floor drains, you ask the owner to have an environmental engineering report available to buyers or tenants.

■ Environmental Issues

Industrial uses of buildings have the potential to create environmental hazards, many of which can move underground. The building across the street, not the one you are selling, may be the cause of the problem. However, your owner is, under current law, responsible for environmental contamination on his property. In today's market, no financial institution will finance a purchase without a satisfactory **environmental report**. Environmental reports are categorized as Phase I, Phase II, and Phase III inspections.

Phase I Inspections

Phase I inspections include the following:

- Site visit—see what's in the neighborhood
- Historical review of site—current and prior uses
- Regulatory review
    - Examines local, state, and federal files
    - For contamination near the site
- Written report
    - OK the property or recommend a Phase II inspection

Every commercial property lender will require a Phase I inspection, which is generally paid for by the property owner. When listing property, discuss the inspection with the owners. Encourage owners to order a Phase I inspection at the time the property is put on the market. If any problems are found, it is easier to address them at this stage—before the sale.

Although it is appropriate to advise all industrial sellers of environmental inspections and recommend that they obtain an environmental report at the time of listing, there may be a problem in doing so. Each lending institution has its own list of approved environmental companies. The buyer's bank or lender may or may not accept an environmental report secured in advance by the seller, so be sure to research approved inspectors before commissioning a report.

As a commercial real estate practitioner, if you suspect an environmental issue at the property being listed—or even from surrounding properties—it is best to bring the issue to the table before the deal gets made.

Many a sale has been lost when an environmental issue is discovered after the negotiations have been completed. Recommend that the owner determine at the time of listing whether there is an environmental issue. Suggest the owner use a major environmental engineering specialist, and remember to find out which banks approve that environmental engineer.

Phase II Inspections

Phase II inspections include the following:

- Soil sampling and laboratory analysis
- Check of groundwater in area around site
- Assesses problems
- Provide possible premediation actions

In a Phase II study, test borings pull soil samples that are tested to determine what chemicals are in the ground and what level of contamination exists. The report will recommend courses of action to deal with the problem. This phase can be relatively expensive, and the cost could become a negotiable item between the seller and the buyer—a price adjustment might occur as a result.

Phase III Inspections

Phase III inspections include the following:

- Action plan for containment or cleanup
- Possible status quo
    - Not to alter existing conditions
- Ongoing monitoring

Phase III deals with the problem. A variety of solutions, which can vary based on the future plans for the site, might be proposed. A property that will be a school in the future may be treated differently than if the land were going to be a parking lot. Sometimes the contaminated soil is dug out and removed; in other cases, it may be capsulated (capped). Often, underground gas station tanks leak, but this may be a minor issue where a filtration monitoring system can satisfactorily handle the problem.

Other extreme cases of environmental pollution are more expensive to clean up than the property is worth. When the cost of cleanup will be high, the property may or may not be worth it. From the broker's point of view, when a property is at a Phase III level, it is a possibility the deal will not close.

■ Marketing of Industrial Properties

When industrial buildings become available, many owners will consider any good business deal and consequently list their property for sale or lease. Buyers of industrial buildings are generally focused on the cost per square foot, and listing flyers will typically quote the purchase price in this manner. User clients compare buying different buildings with the feasibility of new construction by calculating the total cost per square foot. Commercial practitioners should be aware of these things when taking listings and working with these industrial buyers. Tenanted industrial properties also offer an opportunity to market such properties to investors.

Industrial Property Checklist

The Industrial Property Checklist (*see* Figure 4.2) will assist in listing industrial buildings. It is similar in format to the other building checklists presented in the course. It should be used in conjunction with the Listing Information Checklist, which gathers the ownership and contact information. If being sold as an investment property, a financial analysis should also be completed. These checklists are used in addition to a listing agreement.

Note that the building information is to the left and reflects all the items discussed in this chapter. The form calls for type of building. Choose one of the six general categories of industrial buildings: warehouse, factory, manufacturing, distribution, research and development (R&D), and flex space. The building features include items unique to industrial building structures.

Industrial building buyers will focus on the purchase price per square foot. Even though a building's purchase price is recorded on the Listing Information Checklist, for these buildings, it is again entered on line 37, followed by the sales price per square foot on line 38.

Listing industrial buildings may take four forms:

- Sale of the building
- Lease of the entire building
- Lease of part of the building
- Sale of lease of the property

To clarify this point, line 36 on the Industrial Property Checklist (*see* Figure 4.1) indicates whether the property is being marketed for sale or for lease.

Industrial buildings typically do not have common areas and, in many cases, have only one tenant. Consequently, there is usually no distinction between net and gross square footage, which is noted on the checklist with a single line (23) for the rent per square foot. Industrial buildings, however, may have additional rent, in particular when a single-occupant tenant pays the real estate taxes. As with other buildings, the total rent per square foot and the rent per month should be communicated to potential tenants.

Figure 4.1 | Industrial Building Checklist

Building qualities:
1. Type: _____
2. Total size (SF): _____
3. Site size: _____
4. # Floors: _____
5. Year built: _____
6. Construction: _____
7. % Office: _____
8. Freight elevator (Y/N): _____
9. Ceiling height (US): _____
10. Electricity—amps: _____
11. # Overhead doors: _____
12. # Loading docks: _____
13. # Tail-boards: _____
14. Columns (Y/N): _____
15. Sprinklers (Y/N): _____
16. Sewers (Y/N): _____
17. Heat type: _____
18. AC where?: _____
19. # Parking spaces: _____
20. Technical services: _____

If for lease or divisible:
21. Unit #: _____
22. Square footage: _____
23. Rent per SF: _____
Additional rent
24. Utilities per SF: _____
25. CAM per SF: _____
26. Tax per SF: _____
27. Total rent per SF: _____
28. Rent per month: _____
29. Separate electric meter (Y/N): _____
30. NNN lease (Y/N): _____
31. Tax escalation (Y/N): _____
32. ROFR (Y/N): _____
33. Lease term: _____
34. Annual escalations: _____
35. # Assigned parking: _____
36. For sale or lease (Y/N): _____
37. Sale price: _____
38. Sale price per SF: _____

39. Attachments:
    ☐ Survey
    ☐ Floor plans with column placements
    ☐ As-builts
    ☐ Environmental report

40. Features:
    ☐ Refrigeration
    ☐ Freezers
        Describe size and capacity under comments
    ☐ Floor drains

41. Comments:
_____
_____
_____
_____
_____
_____
_____

case study: Industrial Building Checklist

Mrs. Jones, the owner of a commercial warehouse building, calls. She advises you that her tenant is moving to larger quarters and that the property will be available in 60 days. You arrange to meet with her to inspect the building and list the property. At the interview, she advises you that she would either sell or lease the building. On a sale, she wants at least $40.00 per square foot. She will rent it for a minimum of five years for $4.00 per square foot, plus the tenant must pay the taxes, which are $1.85 per square foot. Escalations on a lease would be 3 percent per year. The single-story building is 20,000 square feet and sits on one acre of land. Your physical inspection of the building provides the rest of the information you need. Figure 4.2 shows a completed Industrial Building Checklist depicting all the information you would have gathered.

Figure 4.2 | Completed Industrial Building Checklist

Building qualities:

1. Type: Warehouse
2. Total size (SF): 20,000
3. Site size: 1 acre
4. # Floors: 1
5. Year built: 1985
6. Construction: Masonry
7. % Office: 10%
8. Freight elevator (Y/N): N
9. Ceiling height (US): 18'
10. Electricity—amps: 400
11. # Overhead doors: 1
12. # Loading docks:
13. # Tail-boards: 2
14. Columns (Y/N): Y
15. Sprinklers (Y/N): Y wet
16. Sewers (Y/N): N
17. Heat type: gas
18. AC where?: office only
19. # Parking spaces: 30
20. Technical services: *

If for lease or divisible:

21. Unit #:
22. Square footage: 20,000
23. Rent per SF: $4.00
    Additional rent
24. Utilities per SF:
25. CAM per SF:
26. Tax per SF: $1.85
27. Total rent per SF: $5.85
28. Rent per month: $9,750
29. Separate electric meter (Y/N): Y
30. NNN lease (Y/N): N
31. Tax escalation (Y/N): N
32. ROFR (Y/N): N
33. Lease term: 5+
34. Annual escalations: 3%
35. # Assigned parking:
36. For sale or lease (Y/N): Y
37. Sale price: $800,000
38. Sale price per SF: $40.00

39. Attachments:
    - ☐ Survey
    - ☐ Floor plans with column placements
    - ☐ As-builts
    - ☐ Environmental report

40. Features:
    - ☐ Refrigeration
    - ☐ Freezers
      Describe size and capacity under comments
    - ☐ Floor drains

41. Comments:
    There are no technical services in the building at this time; high-speed phone lines and cable services are available in the area.

Review Questions

1. How is ceiling height referred to in industrial buildings?
   a. Square feet
   b. Floor to ceiling
   c. Under steel
   d. Linear yards

2. Customers who park vehicles in their buildings are concerned with
   a. columns.
   b. loading docks.
   c. ceiling height.
   d. percentage of office.

3. A declining plane or ramp indicates what type of loading facility?
   a. Overhead door
   b. Dock
   c. Tail-board
   d. Roll-off

4. Industrial buildings typically provide what percentage of office space?
   a. 20 percent
   b. 25 percent
   c. 50 percent
   d. 10 percent

5. What technical services might you find in an industrial building?
   a. ISDN
   b. T1–T3
   c. Fiber optics
   d. Any of these

6. A historical site review would be found in what level of environmental report?
   a. Phase I
   b. Phase II
   c. Phase III
   d. Phase IV

7. Remedies for environmental problems might include
   a. capsulation.
   b. doing nothing (status quo).
   c. removing contaminated soil.
   d. all of these.

8. Which type of building is NOT considered industrial?
   a. Flex space
   b. R&D
   c. Auto dealership
   d. Distribution

9. To list an industrial building, what forms do you need?
   a. Building Checklist
   b. Listing agreement
   c. Listing Information Checklist
   d. All of these.

10. What is essential to note on a site inspection?
    a. The neighborhood in which the building is located
    b. Where the building is located on the site
    c. Directions to the property
    d. The number of employees at the building

chapter five

Introduction to Financial Analysis

overview

The retail component of commercial real estate will help us illustrate several new concepts in this chapter. You will be introduced to a form called the Investment Analysis Worksheet, which is designed to organize the data you must collect to establish the value of an investment property. The worksheet uses all the terms and concepts learned so far in this course. In the final section of this chapter, a typical commercial problem, centering on a neighborhood mini mall, provides the opportunity to use the form to help analyze a property. ■

learning objectives

After completing this chapter, you will be able to

- describe how to complete the investment analysis worksheet,
- identify other income sources,
- calculate variable rental incomes,
- perform annual conversions of operating expenses,
- describe the Investment Analysis Worksheet, and
- identify how to calculate market value from raw data.

■ Key Terms

potential rental income   pro forma   replacement reserves

Introduction to Financial Analysis **51**

■ Investment Analysis Worksheet

The Investment Analysis Worksheet (*see* Figure 5.1) is a checklist to accumulate the data needed to calculate net operating income. As you look at the form, you will notice that many of the terms have already been introduced in this course.

The top section of the analysis form records facts about the address, closest cross street, county, tax description, and size. An important instruction follows this section: Enter all figures as annual totals. The form is used to analyze the current year's potential cash flow of the building. It is called a **pro forma**, showing the financial performance of the property in the current year. Most of this information will be supplied by the current property owners or their accountant and will eventually be verified by the potential buyer.

The remainder of the form is divided into three columns: the line item, a column for the dollar amount, and a column for notes and calculations. You use the third column to indicate a conversion note (i.e., if you converted a monthly or per-square-foot cost to an annual charge). For example, rubbish removal is $500 per month. Your entry under contract services would indicate the annual expense of $6,000. Under comments, you would write "$500 per month × 12 months = $6,000 annual cost.

Line-by-Line Review

Remember the worksheet is a checklist. All the entries are explained in the following paragraphs, but note that you will not always have an entry on every line.

- Tenant income. This reflects the potential rental income from the entire rentable square footage of the building. There are three components of potential rental income: actual rent, projection of income from any temporally unoccupied space, and any additional rent the landlord charges the tenants. Additional rent includes things like CAM charges, taxes, or utilities. All of these added together represents the total tenant income.
- Minus: Vacancy contingency (vacancy adjustment). A realistic percentage is determined that represents the amount of space that could become vacant and the length of time it would take to replace a tenant. Even if the building is fully occupied, this contingency addresses the possibility of losing a tenant. On this line, the percentage is entered. It is then multiplied by the total tenant income, and the result is entered as a minus figure in the corresponding center column.
- Adjusted tenant income. This is a subtotal line. Subtract the vacancy contingency amount from the total tenant income and enter the result.
- Other property income. This is other income to the building or property that is not from the tenants. Some examples are as follows:
  - On the roof of an office building—antennas, satellite dishes
  - Billboards
  - Vending machines, pay phones
  - In an apartment building—laundry room, garage rental
- Total gross income (gross operating income). This line totals the income portion of the form.

The next section of the form lists the operating expenses for the property. Record only expenses paid by the owner here; anything paid by tenants are not included in this analysis. The form lists the most common expense categories. You may not

Figure 5.1 | Investment Analysis Worksheet

Location
Street address: _____
City: _____ State: _____ Zip: _____
Closest cross street: _____
County: _____ Section/Block/Lot: _____
Type of property: _____ Size: _____

Enter all figures as annual totals.

Income   **Notes and Calculations**

Tenant income:
   Actual rent: _____ _____
   Projected rent: _____ _____

Additional rent
   CAM: _____ _____
   Taxes: _____ _____
   Utilities: _____ _____
   Other: _____ _____

Total tenant income: _____

Minus: Vacancy contingency

Adjustment (_____ %) _____ _____

Adjusted tenant income: _____ _____

Other property incomes: _____ _____

***Total gross income:** _____ _____

Operating Expenses (Paid by Owner)

Real estate taxes: _____ _____

Insurance: _____ _____

Utilities:
_____ _____ _____
_____ _____ _____
_____ _____ _____

Contract services:
_____ _____ _____
_____ _____ _____
_____ _____ _____

Accounting: _____ _____

Legal: _____ _____

Other professional services: _____ _____

Payroll: _____ _____

Management (_____ %) _____ _____

Repair & maintenance (_____ %) _____ _____

Other:
_____ _____ _____
_____ _____ _____

Total operating expenses: _____

Net operating incomes (NOI): _____

CAP Rate: _____ %   Market value: _____

have an entry for all items listed, and you may have expenses that are not listed. What is important is that all the expenses are accounted for. (Modify the form as needed.)

Tenants may contribute to the cost of some expenses as additional rent, but the owner pays the entire expense. Convert all expenses to annual cost.

- Real estate taxes. Enter the appropriate taxes that are paid by the owner of the property.
- Insurance. Enter annual insurance costs for the property.
- Utilities. These expenses are only for the utilities paid by the owner.
- Contract services. Regular and routine services are listed here. Examples include rubbish collection, cleaning, window washing, landscaping, snow removal etc. Enter any of these expenses on an annual cost basis. These could be services that are billed to the tenants under CAM charges.
- Accounting and legal
- Other professional services
- Payroll
- Management. Often a property management firm of a real estate brokerage company is hired to manage the building or property. This could involve many different levels of responsibilities for different fees. Generally, compensation is in the form of a percentage of the rental income. Be aware that this might be a percentage of gross rent, net rent, actual income—the basis must be defined. If the building has off-site management, unless otherwise specified, calculate the percentage fee based on the rent roll including the actual and projected rent. The additional rent items are not included in this calculation, as these funds are used to pay those bills and are not really income to the landlord.
- Repairs and maintenance. This is a contingency fund for catastrophic events that would require immediate repair or replacement. Examples include roof repairs or HVAC (heating, ventilating, and air-conditioning) problems requiring system replacement. This expense is most often calculated as a percentage of the building's income, but can also be a fixed dollar amount. This is also called **replacement reserves**.

Determining the correct amount of money to set aside for an emergency must be a reality check bases on the actual age and condition of the building. As a guide to selecting a percentage, consider the age and condition of the building(s) and know what responsibilities the owner has for repair and maintenance under the leases. As a rule of thumb, repair and maintenance expenses are usually in the range of 5 percent to 10 percent of the income of the property. Note: When using a percentage, determine whether the owner does the calculation based on the tenant income or the total gross income.

There is a section to enter any other expenses, as follows:

- Total operating expenses (owner's operating expenses). Total all the owner's operating expenses.
- Net operating income. The total gross income less the total operating expenses equals the net operation income.

The final lines of the form are used to enter the prevailing CAP rate and determine market value.

case study: Financial Analysis of Mountain View Mini Mall

Our client owns a neighborhood strip center, called the Mountain View Mini Mall, consisting of six stores with a gross leasable area (GLA) of 10,000 square feet. The site is 40,000 square feet. The rent roll is as follows:

Store	Size	Rent (PSF)
Restaurant	1,500 SF	$15
Dry cleaner	1,500 SF	$15
Video (2 storefronts)	3,000 SF	$18
Stationary shop	2,000 SF	$18
Vacant*	2,000 SF	$16

*Projected rental today. This must be a "reality" number.

All tenants pay additional rent of $1 per square foot in common-area maintenance (CAM) charges.

Landlord's expenses are as follows:

Parking lot cleaning	Per week	$25
Landscaping	Per year	$420
Electricity (sign)	Per month	$50
Insurance	Per year	$6,500
Snow removal	Per year	$500
Rubbish removal	Per month	$150
Accountant	Per year	$1,200
Property taxes	Per year	$52,000

The landlord rarely has vacancies but uses a 5 percent vacancy contingency in his financial statements. He pays a real estate broker 4 percent of his base rent roll to manage the center. The owner puts $10,000 a year into an emergency repair and maintenance fund. There are no other expenses.

Analyze the property using the Investment Analysis Worksheet (Figure 5.1) and develop a market value for the Mountain View Mini Mall based on offering a 12 percent return to the buyer.

Note: Give no consideration to debt service in this exercise.

Calculate the Market Value

To solve this case study, break the problem down into components.

Step 1—Calculate the potential rental income. Potential rental income includes all possible income whether the space is occupied or not (the rent roll), and it includes any "additional Rent" passed through to the tenants.

To begin, each tenant's rent must be calculated to the annual income and then all tenants' income must be totaled.

To calculate the annual rent for each tenant, multiply the square footage occupied times the rent per square foot. For example, with the restaurant tenant calculate as follows:

$$1{,}500 \text{ SF} \times \$15 \text{ PSF} = \$22{,}500 \text{ annual rent.}$$

Base Rent Roll Calculations

Store	SF	×	Base Rent	=	Annual Rent
Restaurant	1,500	×	$15	=	$22,500
Dry Cleaner	1,500	×	$15	=	$22,500
Video	3,000	×	$18	=	$54,000
Stationary	2,000	×	$18	=	$36,000
Total actual rent					$135,000

Next we calculate projected rent for any temporally unoccupied store.

Vacant store	2,000	×	$16	=	$32,000
Total rent roll	10,000 SF				$167,000

The actual rent ($135,000) and projected rent ($32,000) are entered on your worksheet.

Now, add any additional rent paid by the tenants to calculate the total tenant income.

In this problem, the building owner charges the tenants additional rent of $1 per square foot for common-area maintenance (CAM). The total building size is 10,000 square feet. Therefore: 10,000 SF × $1 PSF CAM = $10,000 annual CAM income. Enter this figure under Additional Rent: CAM on the worksheet.

To determine the total tenant income (potential rental income) add together actual rent, **projected rent**, and additional rent, as follows:

$$\$135{,}000 + \$32{,}000 + \$10{,}000 = \$177{,}000$$

The total tenant income is $177,000. Enter this figure on your worksheet.

Step 2—Calculate the vacancy contingency adjustment. The problem tells us to use 5 percent as a vacancy contingency. This is an adjustment to the total tenant income.

Total tenant income	$177,000
Multiplied by 5%	× 0.05
Vacancy contingency	$8,850

Enter the vacancy percentage and $8,850 as a negative number on the analysis worksheet.

When we subtract the dollar amount of the vacancy contingency from the total tenant income, we get the adjusted tenant income.

Total tenant income	$177,000
Less the vacancy contingency	− $8,850
Adjusted tenant income	$168,150

Enter $168,150 on the Adjusted Tenant Income line of the worksheet.

The next line of the form poses the question: Is there any other income to the property not from the tenants? In this problem, there is none; leave this line blank.

The next line is where you record the total gross income (gross operating income). Because in this problem, there is no other property income, the adjusted tenant income will be the same as the total gross income (gross operating income). Enter $168,150 as the total gross income on your form.

Step 3—Calculate the owner's operating expenses. Reread the problem and use the Investment Analysis Worksheet as a checklist to enter the various expenses. Be sure to convert all figures to annual expenses. Then total all the operating expenses.

The total operating expenses are $81,000, calculated as follows:

Real estate taxes	$52,000
Insurance	$6,500
Off-site management (line 9)	$6,680
Utilities:	
Electric	$600

This requires a conversion from a monthly charge of $50 to an annual expense ($50 per month × 12 months = $600 annual expense). Any calculations should be shown in the righthand column under Notes and Calculations.

Contract services:

Cleaning	$1,300
(Based on $25 per week times 52 weeks)	
Landscaping	$420
Snow removal	$500
Rubbish removal	$1,800
(Based on $150 per month times 12 months)	
Accounting	$1,200

Note that in this problem, the owner shows no legal expenses. Ask the owner about any typical building expenses that are missing.

The case study stated that the owner "pays a real estate broker 4 percent of his base rent roll to manage the center." This is a management expense. The base rent roll needs to be defined. The management contract may be based on the rent roll, which may include the potential rental income or be based on only the actual rent collected each month.

Additional rent is never included when calculating the basis for management expenses. You may wonder why the income from the CAM charges is not included; it is generally considered a pass-through expense. For example, the income from CAM charges would be used to pay for the contract services that the charges are based upon. Tax escalations pay part of the tax bill. The landlord never benefits from this money.

In this problem, the management expense was calculated by multiplying the base rent roll by 4 percent ($167,000 × 0.04 = $6,680).

Management $6,680

Repairs and maintenance is a contingency expense usually applied as a percentage of the rental income. But, in some cases, a fixed figure is used. In this case it is $10,000.

As real estate practitioners, we must question the reality of a fixed figure when it is used. If you recall, we previously noted that the typical percentage used in calculating repair and maintenance contingency expenses is between 5 percent and 10 percent. As a comparison, in this problem, if we relate the fixed figure used to the total gross income (gross operating income), we find that is 6 percent, acceptable within the bounds of our reality range.

The repair and maintenance fixed figure is divided by the total gross income ($10,000 ÷ $168,150 = .059 or 6%).

Repair and maintenance $10,000

Added together, the total operating expenses are $81,000.

All the expenses and calculations are entered into the worksheet on their corresponding lines and the total operating expenses are entered.

Step 4—Calculate the net operating income (NOI). The net operating income is the result of subtracting the total operating expenses from the total gross income:

Total gross income	$168,150
Less total operating expenses	−$81,000
Net operating income	$87,150

Enter the NOI on the appropriate line of the Investment Analysis Worksheet.

A completed Investment Analysis Worksheet is shown in Figure 5.2.

Step 5—Calculate the market value of the Mountain View Mini Mall. The problem asks that we calculate the market value of the property based on offering a 12 percent return on the buyer's investment. This is basically the same as a building owner asking, What is my building worth? Given that we know what returns (CAP rates) investors expect in our area, with the NOI, we can now calculate value or price.

To solve this problem for market value, apply the previously learned CAP rate formula as follows:

Net operating income (NOI) $87,150
Capitalization rate (CAP rate)   12%

$$\frac{NOI}{Rate} = Value \qquad \frac{87,150}{0.12} = 726,250$$

Market value $726,250

You have now learned to analyze, with the help of our Investment Analysis Worksheet, a property and have a factual basis to answer the client's question, What is my property worth?

Figure 5.2 | Investment Analysis Worksheet

Location

Street address: _____
City: _____ State: _____ Zip: _____
Closest cross street: ___Second Avenue_____
County: _____ Section/Block/Lot: __4:12:22&23_____
Type of property: __Mini Mall_____ Size: __10,000 SF/5 units_____

Enter all figures as annual totals.

Income		**Notes and Calculations**
Tenant income:		
Actual rent:	$135,000	
Projected rent:	32,000	2,000 SF empty store
Annual rent		
CAM:	10,000	$1 per SF
Taxes:		
Utilities:		
Other:		
Total tenant income:	$177,000	
Minus: Vacancy contingency		
Adjustment (5 %)	− 8,850	
Adjusted tenant income:	168,150	
Other property incomes:		
*Total gross income:	168,150	
Operating Expenses (Paid by Owner)		
Real estate taxes	$52,000	
Insurance:	6,500	
Utilities		
Electric	600	$50 per month (×12)
Contract services:		
Cleaning	1,300	$25 per week (×52)
Landscaping	420	
Snow Removal	500	
Rubbish Removal	1,800	$150 per month (×12)
Accounting:	1,200	
Legal:		
Other professional services:		
Payroll:		
Management (4 %)	6,680	4% of base rent $167,000
Repair & maintenance (5 %)	8,219	5% of gross income
Other:		
Total operating expenses:	$81,000	
Net operating incomes (NOI):	$87,150	
CAP Rate: _____ %		Market value: _____

Review Questions

1. Total tenant income is composed of
   a. actual rent.
   b. potential rent.
   c. additional rent.
   d. all of these.

2. What would be a CAM charge?
   a. Legal expenses
   b. Rubbish removal
   c. Debt service
   d. Property taxes

3. A tax escalation clause could result in
   a. additional rent.
   b. less rent.
   c. increased taxes.
   d. decreased taxes.

4. The total square footage available for lease in a shopping center is known as
   a. CAM.
   b. RET.
   c. PSF.
   d. GLA.

5. Which item would be affected by vacancy?
   a. Vending machines
   b. Roof antennas
   c. CAM charges
   d. Pay phones

6. On the Investment Analysis Worksheet, what is usually calculated as a percentage?
   a. Vacancy and credit losses
   b. Off-site management
   c. Repair and maintenance
   d. All of these

7. Using the Investment Analysis Worksheet, the NOI is determined by subtracting the total operating expenses from what?
   a. Potential rental income
   b. Total gross income
   c. Total tenant income
   d. Annual debt service

8. On the Investment Analysis Worksheet, other property income sources may include
   a. antennas on the roof.
   b. laundry room income from an apartment house.
   c. billboards on the property.
   d. all of these.

9. All dollar figures entered on the Investment Analysis Worksheet reflect
   a. monthly totals.
   b. annual totals.
   c. payment basis used (per week, per month, etc.).
   d. best monthly estimates available.

10. What is the primary purpose of the Investment Analysis Worksheet?
    a. Serve as a checklist to gather and organize data
    b. Determine the property's overall value
    c. Determine market value of a building
    d. Define all possible expenses

chapter six

The Value of Investments

overview

Sometimes, an investor can make more money by using other people's money as part of the investment strategy. "Other people's money" might simply be a bank mortgage, or it may involve gathering a group of other investors, or partners, for the project.

Many different terms are used to describe the value of an investment to the owner or to a potential purchaser. ∎

learning objectives

After completing this chapter, you will be able to

- define rate of return,
- analyze cash flow before taxes (CFBT),
- calculate cash-on-cash returns,
- describe the impact of leveraging on the cash-on-cash return, and
- describe the concept of internal rate of return (IRR).

∎ Key Terms

annual property operating data (APOD)
cash flow before taxes (CFBT)
cash-on-cash return
equity
initial investment
internal rate of return (IRR)
leverage
rate of return

Investment Strategies

In Chapter 1, we looked at the capitalization rate (CAP rate) as an investor's desired profit percentage, which is used to project the property value. This chapter will focus primarily on a building's current owner, work with the actual sale prices of property, and determine existing rates of return. But before we explore investment strategies, we must first define some key terms.

Important Investment Terms

The following terms are often used when discussing real estate investments.

- **Rate of return**—The percentage return on each dollar invested. This is also known as the yield.
- **Leverage**—The use of borrowed funds to finance a portion of the cost of an investment. Typically this is in the form of a mortgage on the property. The annual expense of a mortgage, including principal and interest, is called annual debt service.
- **Initial investment**—The down payment. The sales price plus acquisition costs less the amount of the mortgage loan is the down payment.
- **Cash flow before taxes (CFBT)**—The net operating income (NOI) less the annual debt service equals cash flow before taxes.
- **Equity**—The value of one's interest in the property, equity consists of fair market value less any outstanding debt or other encumbrances. It generally increases as the mortgage balance decreases.
- **Cash-on-cash return**—A simple return measure. It is calculated as cash flow before taxes (CFBT) divided by the initial investment.
- **Internal rate of return (IRR)**—A calculation that covers the entire life of the investment and in essence shows the average annual return for the entire holding period. This mathematically complex calculation is the discount rate at which the present value of future cash flows is exactly equal to the initial capital investment.

Learning IRR calculations is material for an advanced investment course. It is only mentioned here so the student is aware that there are other methods used by investors to evaluate investment properties.

Comparison of Investment Methods

All Cash Purchase

In the final problem in Chapter 5, we determined that, based on a 12 percent CAP rate, the market value of the six-store strip center known as the Mountain View Mini Mall to be $726,250.

An investor who bought the property for $726,250, all cash, would have after the first year a 12 percent return on investment (ROI) of $87,150 (NOI) before taxes.

Leveraged Purchase

Assume the buyer of the mini mall financed the purchase by obtaining a bank mortgage and leveraging the purchase. What would be the buyer's cash-on-cash return?

To determine cash-on-cash return, it is necessary to apply the definitions learned in this chapter and to know the terms of the of the bank mortgage.

The relevant formulas are:

Cash flow before taxes = Net operating income − Annual debt service

$$\begin{aligned}&\text{NOI}\ \ (\text{net operating income})\\&\underline{-\ \text{ADS}\ \ (\text{annual debt service})}\\&\text{CFBT}\ \ (\text{cash flow before taxes})\end{aligned}$$

Cash on cash return = Cash flow before taxes ÷ Initial investment

$$\frac{\text{CFBT (cash flow before taxes)}}{\text{II (initial investment)}} = \text{Cash-on-cash return}$$

In order to determine cash-on-cash returns, we must first calculate the cash flow before taxes. From our last problem, we know the following:

Sales price	$726,250
NOI (net operating income)	$87,150

For purposes of this comparison, make the following mortgage assumptions: 15-year term, 7.5 percent interest, and 25 percent down payment, with monthly payments. Based on these assumptions, the annual debt service can be calculated:

Sales price	$726,250
Down payment (25%)	$181,562
Mortgage amount	$544,688
Annual debt service	$60,592

We now have all the figures required to calculate the cash-on-cash return, as follows:

Step 1—Calculate the CFBT (cash flow before taxes)

Net Operating Income (NOI)	$87,150
Annual debt service	− $60,592
Cash flow before taxes (CFBT)	$26,558

Step 2—Calculate the cash-on-cash return

$$\frac{\text{CFBT}}{\text{Initial investment}} = \text{Cash-on-cash return}$$

$$\frac{\$26{,}558\ (\text{CFBT})}{\$181{,}562\ (\text{initial investment})} = 0.1463\ (14.6\%)\ \text{cash-on-cash return}$$

In this case, leveraging increased the investor's return from 12 percent return on investment (ROI) in the all-cash purchase example to 14.6 percent cash-on-cash return. Also, by leveraging this purchase, the investor would have still have $544,688 from his original cash supply to make other investments.

Note: The interest rate and terms of the mortgage will affect the cash-on-cash return. This could, in some cases, make the all-cash purchase ROI a higher overall return. Potential investment returns should be evaluated both ways.

Figure 6.1 | Investment Strategies

Investment Strategy	Attributes
Stability	Stable building, fully rented; reasonable return
Potential	Building requires upgrading; future potential for a higher return
Flipping	Buy depressed properties; fix up; sell quickly (or flip) at profit
Upside Potential	Good building, old leases, low current rents; replace tenants
Holder	Buy for the long term; never sell

Investor Strategies

Investors have their own individual goals with investment properties. Different strategies may cause investors to focus on certain criteria for their purchases, as noted in Figure 6.1.

Investors may have many considerations and goals in choosing the properties they buy. As a broker, discuss with your investor clients their particular selection strategy. It will help you service them better.

Most investors seek immediate cash flow profits from their properties. Some prefer that they never have to add money to their investment because of vacancies and the consequent lack of income. As an example, an investor buys buildings with 25 percent down and seeks 15-year mortgages. His only criteria is that the NOI is sufficient to pay the debt service on the building. In so doing, his required rent to break even is usually below market, and he literally never has any vacancies in his buildings.

In 15 years, when this investor retires, all his mortgages will start to be paid off and the income from his building will be his retirement fund. This will allow him to live comfortably on his income and pass the building ownership to his family.

Know the goals of your investors. It will help you find the right property for them.

■ CCIM—Certified Commercial Investment Member

The CCIM Institute is affiliated with the National Association of REALTORS® and provides extensive educational courses leading to attaining the Certified Commercial Investment Member designation.

The institute uses a form similar to the Investment Analysis Worksheet called an **annual property operating data (APOD)** sheet. Figure 6.2 shows a completed APOD based on the Mountain View Mini Mall case study in the previous chapter.

The form can be used for multiple purposes, such as determining NOI or showing a cash flow before tax. At the top and bottom of the form, there is an area for entering current or proposed mortgage information. Below the NOI are lines for the annual debt service and other adjustments. The form concludes with the cash flow before taxes entry. Another major difference is that this form combines all the tenant income (actual, projected, and additional rent) into one line called Potential Rental Income.

Figure 6.2 | Annual Property Operating Data

Annual Property Operating Data

Property Name: Mini Mall
Location:
Type of Property: Retail Strip
Size of Property: 10,000 SF/6 (Sq. Ft./Units)

Purpose of analysis:

Assessed/Appraised Values
Land
Improvements
Personal Property
Total

Adjusted Basis as of:

Purchase Price
Plus Acquisiition Costs
Plus Loan Fees/Costs
Less Mortgages
Equals Initial Investment

	Balance	Periodic Pmt	Pmts/Yr	Interest	Amort Period	Loan Term
1st			12			
2nd			12			

#	ALL FIGURES ARE ANNUAL	$/SQ FT or $/Unit	% of GOI		Balance	COMMENTS/FOOTNOTES
1	**POTENTIAL RENTAL INCOME**				177,000	Base Rent $167,000 + $10,000 CAM
2	Less: Vacancy & Cr. Losses			(5% of PRI)	8,850	
3	**EFFECTIVE RENTAL INCOME**				168,150	
4	Plus: Other Income (collectable)					
5	**GROSS OPERATING INCOME**				168,150	
	OPERATING EXPENSES:					
7	Real Estate Taxes				52,000	
8	Personal Property Taxes					
9	Property Insurance				6,500	
10	Off Site Management				6,680	4% of Base Rent $167,000
11	Payroll					
12	Expenses/Benefits					
13	Taxes/Worker's Compensation					
14	Repairs and Maintenance				10,000	
	Utilities:					
15	Electric				600	$50 month (X12)
16						
17						
18						
19	Accounting and Legal				1,200	
20	Licenses/Permits					
21	Advertising					
22	Supplies					
23	Miscellaneous Contract Services:					
24	Cleaning				1,300	$25 week (X52)
25	Landscaping				420	
26	Snow Removal				500	
27	Rubbish Removal				1,800	$150 month (X12)
28						
29	TOTAL OPERATING EXPENSES				81,000	
30	**NET OPERATING INCOME**				87,150	
31	Less: Annual Debt Service					
32	Less: Participation Payments					
33	Less: Leasing Commissions					
34	Less: Funded Reserves					
35	**CASH FLOW BEFORE TAXES**					

Copyright © 2012 by the CCIM Institute

The statements and figures herein, while not guaranteed, are secured from sources we believe authoritative.

Prepared for:
Prepared by:

Review Questions

1. Leveraging is
   a. a guarantee of a higher yield.
   b. the use of borrowed funds to finance a portion of the cost of an investment.
   c. net operating income less the annual debt service.
   d. the fair market value less any outstanding debt or encumbrances.

2. The method for determining the cash-on-cash return is
   a. subtract the debt service from the net operating income.
   b. divide the cash flow before taxes by the initial investment.
   c. subtract the down payment from the sales price.
   d. divide the initial investment by the return on investment.

3. The net operating income less the annual debt service is
   a. investment return.
   b. cash-on-cash return.
   c. cash flow before taxes.
   d. the equity.

4. A calculation that considers the entire life of the investment is
   a. cash-on-cash return.
   b. return on investment.
   c. leveraging.
   d. internal rate of return.

5. The desired profit percentage of an investor is called
   a. CAP rate.
   b. ROI.
   c. NOI.
   d. CFBT.

6. The annual debt service figure is necessary for calculating
   a. initial investment.
   b. return on investment.
   c. yield.
   d. cash flow before taxes.

7. Leveraging
   a. always increases the return on an investment.
   b. never effects the return on an investment.
   c. requires the CAP rate for calculation.
   d. may increase returns on investments depending on rates and terms of the financing.

8. A property has a net operating income of $67,500, and an investor offers $450,000, all cash, to purchase it. What return on investment is that investor expecting?
   a. 6.67 percent
   b. 15 percent
   c. 12.5 percent
   d. None of these

9. A property has net operating income of $67,500, and an investor offers $450,000 to purchase it with a down payment of $100,000. The annual debt service for the mortgage is $38,934. What is the buyer's anticipated cash-on-cash return?
   a. 39 percent
   b. 29 percent
   c. 6 percent
   d. 8 percent

10. If in question 9, the down payment was increased to $200,000, the cash-on-cash return would
    a. increase.
    b. decrease.
    c. remain the same.
    d. become zero.

chapter seven

Forecasting Cash Flows

overview

This chapter consists of four different ways to analyze an office building. It begins with the current year analysis, expands to a five-year review, and looks at value from both the owner's and the buyer's perspective. You will learn to project the future income of properties, its effect on value, and how investors think. ∎

learning objectives

After completing this chapter, you will be able to

- describe the use of the Investment Analysis Worksheet,
- describe the effects of leveraging,
- summarize the impact of up-side events,
- measure rent escalations,
- describe how to develop five-year property projections,
- identify different returns on investments,
- describe how to determine market value, and
- recognize the key assumptions on which to negotiate.

■ Key Terms

comparable sales approach
cost approach
income approach
lease extract
spreadsheet
upside potential

Current Year Analysis

Forecasting Cash Flows

To properly present an investment opportunity for a property with **upside potential**, the cash flow must be projected for future years. This is generally done with a five-year analysis, but a longer term can be used, if appropriate.

case study	**Small Office Building**

The following problem will demonstrate how to develop a five-year projection of a small office building. Mr. Smith, the client, owns a building and wants to put it on the market for sale. His question is, "What is my building worth?"

To answer this question, it will be necessary to do a financial analysis for year 1 and make adjustments to the income and expenses for the next four years. Creating current and projected net operating incomes (NOI) will provide a basis for value.

If existing debt service is factored in, cash-on-cash returns can be determined over the five-year period, showing value from the owner's point of view.

This exercise extends over the entire chapter and involves many of the concepts learned in this course. It is a real-world problem of the kind typically encountered by commercial/investment brokers every day.

case study	**Mr. Smith's Office**

It is December of the current year. Mr. Smith called you and said he wanted to sell his office building. He asked you to stop by and tell him what it is worth.

You advised him that before you could do that, you would need a summary of the leases (or actual leases) and all the expenses for the building. In addition, he would need to answer certain questions for you. An interview is arranged, and you meet and gather the data you need for evaluation. A synopsis of the relevant facts follows.

Building description is as follows:

- Three-story Class B office building with elevator
- Gross leasable area of 2,500 square feet on each floor
- A 1,200-square-foot leasable area in the lower level, which is presently the only vacancy in the building
- Roof space leased to a phone company for an antenna

The gross square footage leased to each tenant and the lease terms are displayed in Figure 7.1.

This type of spreadsheet is known as a **lease extract**. It offers a summary of all the leases in a building showing commencement and ending dates, escalations, current rent, additional rent, and options.

Figure 7.1 | Lease Extract Spreadsheet

Tenant	Rentable SF	Current Rent $	Lease Start Date	Lease End Date	Escalations %	Options
Shoe	2,500	14	Jan. 10 years ago	December current year	2	None
Pizza	1,250	18	May 4 years ago	May next year	3	5 year
Cleaner	1,250	19	March 6 years ago	March 4 years from now	4	10 year
Bank	1,500	19	Jan, 2 years ago	January 18 years from now	10 (every 5 years)	None
Clothing	1,000	20	June 1 year ago	June 9 years from now	3	Two, 5 year
Vacant	1,200	10				

Other building considerations include the following:

- There is an agreement that allows a phone company to have a relay antenna on the roof for a fee of $500 per month.
- The owner uses 7 percent as a vacancy adjustment, 5 percent for repair contingency based on the gross operating income, and manages the building himself.
- Taxes are presently $50,000 per year but have just been reduced. The tax reductions are effective as follows: $2,500 in two years, a further reduction of $2,500 in the year after that.
- All other operating expenses combined are presently $20,000 and are expected to increase at a rate of 3 percent per year.
- The current owner bought the building five years ago for $500,000. He paid $125,000 cash down and financed $375,000 at 9 percent interest (fixed rate) for 15 years. Annual mortgage payments are $45,642.

Office Building Problem—Part A

Complete an Investment Analysis Worksheet to determine the NOI, and then determine the cash-on-cash return on the building.

Hint: Information has been provided that you do not need for this part of the problem. You are only concerned, in this part, with the current year's income and expenses. Do the problem in components, using the Investment Analysis Worksheet (*see* Figure 7.2) as a checklist.

Part A Solution

Step 1—Complete the top portion of the worksheet.

Use the blank Investment Analysis Worksheet in Figure 7.2 for this problem.

Based on the facts stated in the problem, enter the following information:

    Type of Property: Office Building Class B
    Size of Property: 8,700 SF / 6 units

Figure 7.2 | Investment Analysis Worksheet

Location
Street address: _____
City: _____ State: _____ Zip: _____
Closest cross street: _____
County: _____ Section/Block/Lot: _____
Type of property: _____ Size: _____

Enter all figures as annual totals.

Income		**Notes and Calculations**

Tenant income:
   Actual rent: _____ _____
   Projected rent: _____ _____
Additional rent
   CAM: _____ _____
   Taxes: _____ _____
   Utilities: _____ _____
   Other: _____ _____
Total tenant income: _____ _____
Minus: Vacancy contingency
Adjustment (_____ %) _____ _____
Adjusted tenant income: _____ _____
Other property incomes: _____ _____
*Total gross income: _____ _____

Operating Expenses (Paid by Owner)
Real estate taxes: _____ _____
Insurance: _____ _____
Utilities:
_____ _____ _____
_____ _____ _____
_____ _____ _____

Contract services:
_____ _____ _____
_____ _____ _____
_____ _____ _____
_____ _____ _____

Accounting: _____ _____
Legal: _____ _____
Other professional services: _____ _____
Payroll: _____ _____
Management (_____ %) _____ _____
Repair & maintenance (_____ %) _____ _____
Other:
_____ _____ _____
_____ _____ _____

Total operating expenses: _____
Net operating incomes (NOI): _____
CAP Rate: _____ %   Market value: _____

Step 2—Determine the current rent roll, and enter the tenant income on the form.

The current rent roll is determined by first multiplying each tenant's gross square footage (GSF) by the rent per square foot (PSF) to calculate each tenant's annual rent. All the tenants' incomes are then added together. All rentable space is considered, whether occupied or not.

Tenant	GLA	Rent PSF $	Annual Rent $
A	2,500	14	35,000
B	1,250	18	22,500
C	1,250	19	23,750
D	1,500	19	28,500
E	1,000	20	20,000
F (projected)	1,200	10	12,000

Next, any additional rent collected by the landlord (e.g., CAM charges, tax escalations) is added to the rent roll. The total is the total tenant income (potential rental income). In this problem, there is no additional rent charged.

The income section of the worksheet should show these figures:

Income

Tenant Income:		
Actual Rent:	$129,750	
Projected Rent:	12,000	(1,200 SF LL at $10 PSF)
Additional Rent:		(There is no additional rent in this problem.)
Total Tenant Income:	$141,750	

Step 3—Complete the other income portions of the worksheet.

The next part of our analysis calls for calculating vacancy contingency; in this problem, the owner uses 7 percent as a vacancy contingency. Take 7 percent of the total tenant income to determine the vacancy adjustment. $141,750 × 0.07 = $9,922.50, rounded to $9,923.

Adjusted Tenant Income results from subtracting the dollar amount of the vacancy adjustment from the total rental income. $141,750 – $9,923 = $131,827.

The next line on the worksheet asks whether there is any other property income. In this case, there is income from the roof antenna in the amount to $500 per month. This must be converted to an annual figure. $500 × 12 = $6,000.

To complete the income section and determine the total gross income, add the adjusted tenant income and the other property income: $131,827 + $6,000 = $137,827. (*See* Figure 7.3.)

Figure 7.3 | Total Gross Income

Income	Notes and Calculations	
Tenant income:		
Actual rent:	$129,750	
Projected rent:	12,000	1,200 SF LL at $10 PSF
Annual rent		
CAM:		
Taxes:		
Utilities:		
Other:		
Total tenant income:	$141,750	
Minus: Vacancy contingency		
Adjustment (7 %)	– 9,923	$141,750 × .07 = 9,922.50
Adjusted tenant income:	131,827	
Other property incomes:	6,000	$500 × 12 = $6,000
*Total gross income:	$137,827	

Step 4—Enter the operating expenses on the Investment Analysis Worksheet.

In this problem, there are only three expenses:

Real estate taxes:	$50,000
Repairs and maintenance:	$6,891
The repairs and maintenance are stated by the owner to be 5 percent of gross operating income.	$137,827 × 0.05 = $6,891

All other expenses: $20,000 (enter this amount under Other)

Total operating expenses is determined by adding all three expenses: $76,891

Step 5—Determine the net operating income (NOI).

The NOI is equal to the total gross income minus the total operating expenses.

$$\$137,827 - \$76,891 = \$60,936 \text{ (NOI)}$$

This data should be entered on the worksheet (*see* Figure 7.4).

The next section of this part of the problem asks you to determine the owner's current cash-on-cash return. In order to do so, you must first calculate the cash flow before taxes by subtracting the annual debt service from the new operating income.

Figure 7.4 | Completed Investment Analysis Worksheet

Location
Street address: _____
City: _____ State: _____ Zip: _____
Closest cross street: _____
County: _____ Section/Block/Lot: _____
Type of property: _____ Size: _____

Enter all figures as annual totals.

Income		**Notes and Calculations**
Tenant income:		
Actual rent:	$129,750	
Projected rent:	12,000	1,200 SF LL at $10 PSF
Additional rent		
CAM:		
Taxes:		
Utilities:		
Other:		
Total tenant income:	$141,750	
Minus: Vacancy contingency		
Adjustment (7 %)	− 9,923	$141,750 × .07 = 9,922.50
Adjusted tenant income:	131,827	
Other property incomes:	6,000	$500 × 12 = 6,000
*Total gross income:	$137,827	
Operating Expenses (Paid by Owner)		
Real estate taxes:	$50,000	
Insurance:		
Utilities:		
Contract services:		
Accounting:		
Legal:		
Other professional services:		
Payroll:		
Management (____ %)		
Repair & maintenance (5 %)	6,891	$137,837 × .05 = 6,891
Other:		
All Other Expenses	20,000	
Total operating expenses:	76,901	
Net operating incomes (NOI):	$60,936	
CAP Rate: _____ %		Market value: _____

The problem gave us the following mortgage information:

- The owner purchased the property five years ago for $500,000, with a down payment (or initial investment) of $125,000.
- A fixed-rate mortgage was secured with annual payments (annual debt service) of $45,642.

Step 6—Determine the cash flow before taxes (CFBT).

The cash flow before taxes is determined by subtracting the annual debt service from the net operating income.

Net operating income	$60,936
Less annual debt service	– $45,642
Equals cash flow before taxes	$15,294

Step 7—Determine the cash-on-cash return.

$$\frac{\text{Cash flow before taxes}}{\text{Initial investment}} = \text{Cash-on-cash return}$$

The initial investment is the down payment.

$$\frac{\$15{,}294 \text{ (CFBT)}}{\$125{,}000 \text{ (initial investment)}} = 0.1224 \text{ (12.24 percent cash-on-cash return)}$$

This works out to a 12.24 percent return on the investment today, five years after the purchase. One would have expected a higher rate of return after holding a property for five years. The problem with the bottom line on this investment is largely caused by the 9 percent mortgage interest rate. If you recall the leveraging example in Chapter 6, leveraging brought the cash-on-cash return up to 14 percent, as opposed to an all-cash purchase of 12 percent. But the interest rate in the earlier example was 7.5 percent. It is important to note that, based upon the economy and prevailing interest rates, the effects of leveraging on the bottom line (the profit of the investment) will vary.

The problem stated that the owner bought the building five years ago. If he had bought the building all cash for $500,000, what would his return be today? Use the capitalization rate formula to determine this.

$$\frac{\text{Net operating income}}{\text{Value (Purchase Price)}} = \text{Capitalization rate}$$

$$\frac{\$60{,}936 \text{ (NOI)}}{\$500{,}000 \text{ (value)}} = 0.1219 \text{ (12.19 percent CAP rate)}$$

At this time, without debt servicing, the property would give the owner more than a 12 percent return on the investment, about the same as leveraging at the high interest rate. However, by leveraging the property, the cash outlay (down payment) at the time of purchase was $125,000. Assuming the current owner had $500,000 to spend when he bought the building, leveraging would have allowed him to acquire other investments. He might have accepted a lower rate of return on some, such as this property, that he believed had good upside potential.

The Spreadsheet

In order to give a potential buyer a clear picture of a purchase opportunity, including return on investment and upside potential, it is often necessary to do a five-year (or longer) forecast of cash flows. In essence, you are creating five Investment Analysis Worksheets (one for each year), but rather than use that format, you create a **spreadsheet**.

Office Building Problem Part B

Create a five-year spreadsheet showing the cash flow before taxes on the office building.

This part of the problem is done in two sections, the first being to develop the potential rental income (total tenant income) for each year. To accomplish this, each individual lease must be examined and the rent escalations (increases) for each year calculated.

From Part A of the problem, the current year's rent roll is known. It has been entered on the following spreadsheet (Figure 7.5). Complete the form by adding the appropriate rent increases to each tenant's anticipated annual rent.

The lease terms and increases must now be examined. These are shown in Figure 7.6.

Read the lease notes that follow and complete the spreadsheet in Figure 7.5, solving for the potential rental income each year. Remember the time frame of this problem: December of the current year.

Lease Notes

- **Tenant A:** Occupies 2,500 square feet; the lease expires December of this year. Current rent is $14 per square foot. Annual escalations are irrelevant as the lease is expiring. Note: Current average rent in the building is $19 per square foot and escalations average 3 percent.

  This is an old lease that expires at the end of this month. The tenant will either renew the lease at the market rate or be asked to leave. It is a reasonable assumption that a new lease (starting next month) will be at fair market value, the average rent level, and terms as the rest of the building.

Figure 7.5 | Potential Rental Income Spreadsheet

Section 1—Calculate potential rental income for each year.

Tenant	Current Year $	Year 2 $	Year 3 $	Year 4 $	Year 5 $
A	35,000	_____	_____	_____	_____
B	22,500	_____	_____	_____	_____
C	23,750	_____	_____	_____	_____
D	28,500	_____	_____	_____	_____
E	20,000	_____	_____	_____	_____
F	12,000	_____	_____	_____	_____
Total	141,750	_____	_____	_____	_____

Figure 7.6 | Lease Terms and Increases

Tenant	Rentable SF	Current Rent $	Lease Start Date	Lease End Date	Escalations %	Options
A. Shoe	2,500	14	January 10 years ago	December current year	2	None
B. Pizza	1,250	18	May 4 years ago	May next year	3	5 year
C. Cleaner	1,250	19	March 6 years ago	March 4 years from now	4	10 year
D. Bank	1,500	19	January 2 years ago	January 18 years from now	10 (every 5 years)	None
E. Clothing	1,000	20	June 1 year ago	June 9 years from now	3	Two, 5 year
F. Vacant	1,200	10				

- **Tenant B:** Occupies 1,250 square feet; the lease expires next year. Current rent is $18 per square foot. Annual escalations are 3 percent.
- **Tenant C:** Occupies 1,250 square feet; lease expires in four years. Current rent is $19 per square foot. Annual escalations are 4 percent.
- **Tenant D:** Occupies 1,500 square feet; the lease started two years ago and expires in 13 years. Current rent is $19 per square foot. Escalations are 10 percent every five years. Because the lease started only two years ago, the first five-year increase will not occur for another three years.
- **Tenant E:** Occupies 1,000 square feet; lease expires in nine years. Current rent is $20 per square foot. Annual escalations are 3 percent.
- **Tenant F:** Vacant space of 1,000 square feet in the lower level. Projected rent is $10 per square foot. Projected escalations are 3 percent. Assume this space will be rented in January.

A recap of the problem adjustments is as follows:

- There is an agreement that allows a phone company to have a relay antenna on the roof for a fee of $500 per month.

Figure 7.7 | Office Building Problem Part B Solution

Section 1—Determine potential rental income for each year.

Tenant	Current Year $	Year 2 $	Year 3 $	Year 4 $	Year 5 $
A	35,000	47,500	48,925	50,393	51,905
B	22,500	23,175	23,870	24,586	25,324
C	23,750	24,700	25,688	26,716	27,784
D	28,500	28,500	28,500	31,350	31,350
E	20,000	20,600	21,218	21,855	22,500
F	12,000	12,360	12,731	13,113	13,506
Total	141,750	156,835	160,932	168,013	172,379

- The owner uses 7 percent as a vacancy adjustment, 5 percent for repair contingency based on the gross operating income, and manages the building himself.
- Taxes are presently $50,000 per year but have just been reduced. The tax reductions are effective as follows: a reduction of $2,500 in year 3, a further reduction of $2,500 in year 4.
- All other operating expenses combine presently to $20,000 and are expected to increase at a rate of 3 percent per year.

Tenant A. Because the lease expired in December of the current year, there is no rent escalation to calculate for the next year. Rather, a new lease starts in January (year 2), which is based on fair market value (average rent in the building of $19 per square foot). The rent for year 2 is calculated: 2,500 SF × $19 PSF = $47,500.

The average rent escalations in the building are 3 percent, which will be used for this new lease.

Each year thereafter will be calculated as 1.03 times the previous year's rent, as follows:

- Year 3 rent: $47,500 (prior year's rent) × 1.03 = $48,925
- Year 4 rent: $48,925 (prior year's rent) × 1.03 = $50,393
- Year 5 rent: $50,393 (prior year's rent) × 1.03 = $51,905

Tenant B. This lease started four years ago and ends next year. Rent increases 3 percent per year. In this case, the tenant has a five-year option to continue the lease. Assume the option will be executed and continue with the 3 percent annual increase in the projections as follow:

- Year 2 rent: $22,500 (current year rent) × 1.03 = $23,175
- Year 3 rent: $23,175 (prior year's rent) × 1.03 = $23,870
- Year 4 rent: $23,870 × 1.03 = $24,586
- Year 5 rent: $24,586 × 1.03 = $25,324

Tenant C. This lease started six years ago and ends in the last year of the projections. Rent increases 4 percent per year, as shown:

- Year 2 rent: $23,750 (prior year's rent) × 1.04 = $24,700
- Year 3 rent: $24,700 × 1.04 = $25,688
- Year 4 rent: $25,688 × 1.04 = $26,716
- Year 5 rent: $26,716 × 1.04 = $27,784

Tenant D. This lease has a rent escalation that occurs every five years. The lease started 2 years ago and runs another 18 years. During the five-year analysis, a rent increase is due in year 4.

The current rent of $28,500 remains the same for years 2 and 3. The year 4 rent increases by 10 percent.

- Year 3 rent: $28,500 (prior year's rent) × 1.10 = $31,350

The next escalation in this lease occurs in year 10 of the lease; therefore, the rent in year 5 is the same as the year 4 rent.

Tenant E. This lease started last year and continues beyond the projection period. Rent increases 3 percent per year.

- Year 2 rent: $20,000 (prior year's rent) × 1.03 = $20,600
- Year 3 rent: $20,600 × 1.03 = $21,218
- Year 4 rent: $21,218 × 1.03 = $21,855
- Year 5 rent: $21,855 × 1.03 = $22,510

Tenant F. This is vacant space. However, when calculating potential rental income, rent is projected for all space, whether occupied or not. For purposes of this problem, the current rent was projected as $12,000, based on the average increase of 3 percent. In the case study, it was assumed that when the space is rented in the next year, rent will be 3 percent higher, as follows:

- Year 2 rent: $12,000 (prior year's projected rent) × 1.03 = $12,360
- Year 3 rent: $12,360 (2000 rent) × 1.03 = $12,731
- Year 4 rent: $12,731 × 1.03 = $13,113
- Year 5 rent: $13,113 × 1.03 = $13,506

The projected rents from each tenant for each year are added together to produce the five-year projected rental incomes.

The potential rental income. Determined in the first section of this part, this amount is entered across line 1 of the spreadsheet. Just like the Investment Analysis Worksheet, the amount for each line is calculated for each year.

Vacancy adjustment. The problem states that a 7 percent adjustment is made for vacancy. Multiply the potential rental income for each year by 0.07 to calculate the dollar value of the vacancy adjustment, as follows:

Current year: $141,750 × 0.07 = $9,923
Year 2: $156,835 × 0.07 = $10,978
Year 3: $160,932 × 0.07 = $11,265
Year 4: $168,013 × 0.07 = $11,761
Year 5: $172,379 × 0.07 = $12,067

The results are entered on line 2 of the chart.

Other income. The problem has other income (not affected by vacancy), which is the antenna fee of $6,000 per year. This figure is inserted for each year under Other Income on the spreadsheet.

Gross operating income. This is the total, by year, of the previous entries. The vacancy adjustment is subtracted from the potential rental income. The other income is added to that figure, and the result is the gross operating income.

For example, this is the current year's calculation:

Potential rental income	$141,750
Less vacancy adjustment	− 9,923
(Subtotal)	131,827
Plus other income	+ 6,000
Gross operating income	$137,827

Expenses

Taxes. Current taxes are $50,000 per year; this amount remains constant until year 3 when taxes will be reduced by $2,500 to $47,500. The taxes were reduced again in year 4 by another $2,500 to $45,000, an amount that remains the same for year 5.

Repairs and maintenance. This contingency expense is being calculated in this problem as 5 percent of the gross operating income.

Just a reminder, some investors may take the percentage from the potential rental income or the effective rental income instead of the gross operating income. Some may use a fixed dollar amount. Clarify the basis of this calculation so that everyone is making the calculation the same way.

For this problem, multiply the gross operating income for each year by 5 percent.

    Current year: $137,827 × 0.05 = $6,891
    Year 2: $151,857 × 0.05 = $7,593
    Year 3: $155,667 × 0.05 = $7,783
    Year 4: $162,252 × 0.05 = $8,113
    Year 5: $166,312 × 0.05 = $8,316

Remaining expenses. In this problem, all other expenses were lumped together as a single entry of $20,000 in the current year. These expenses are projected to increase by 3 percent each year.

To calculate the next year's expenses, multiply the current year by 1.03.

Figure 7.8 | Cash Flow Before Taxes

Section 2—Calculate the cash flow before taxes (CFBT).

Once the potential rental income for each year is known, that year's adjustments and expenses can be calculated to determine NOI and cash flow before taxes. The spreadsheet concept is again used. Fill in the spreadsheet using the information from the lease notes.

	Current Year $	Year 2 $	Year 3 $	Year 4 $	Year 5 $
Potential rental income	141,750	_____	_____	_____	_____
Vacancy adjustment	_____	_____	_____	_____	_____
Other income	_____	_____	_____	_____	_____
Gross operating income	_____	_____	_____	_____	_____
Expenses:					
Taxes	_____	_____	_____	_____	_____
Repair and maintenance	_____	_____	_____	_____	_____
All other expenses	_____	_____	_____	_____	_____
Total expenses	_____	_____	_____	_____	_____
Net operating income	_____	_____	_____	_____	_____
Debt service	_____	_____	_____	_____	_____
Cash flow before taxes	_____	_____	_____	_____	_____

Figure 7.9 | Section 2—Cash Flow Before Taxes (CFBT)

	Current Yr. $	Year 2 $	Year 3 $	Year 4 $	Year 5 $
Potential rental income	141,750	156,835	160,932	168,013	172,379
Vacancy adjustment	9,923	10,978	11,265	11,791	12,067
Other income	6,000	6,000	6,000	6,000	6,000
Gross operating income	137,827	151,857	155,667	162,252	166,312
Expenses:					
Taxes	50,000	50,000	47,500	45,000	45,000
Repair and maintenance	6,891	7,593	7,783	8,113	8,316
All other expenses	20,000	20,600	21,218	21,885	22,510
Total expenses	76,891	78,193	76,501	74,968	75,826
NOI	60,936	73,664	79,166	87,284	90,486
Debt service	45,642	45,642	45,642	45,642	45,642
Cash flow before taxes	15,294	28,022	33,524	41,642	44,844

Current year:	$20,000
Year 2:	$20,000 × 1.03 = $20,600
Year 3:	$20,600 × 1.03 = $21,218
Year 4:	$21,218 × 1.03 = $21,885
Year 5:	$21,885 × 1.03 = $22,510

Total expenses. All expenses by year are now totaled.

Net operating income. For each year, subtract the total expenses from the gross operating income to calculate the NOI.

Cash flow before taxes (CFBT). This is determined by subtracting the annual debt service from the net operating income.

For example, the first year's calculation looks like this:

Gross operating income	$137,827
Less total expenses	− 76,891
Net operating income	60,936
Less annual debt service	− 45,642
Cash flow before taxes	$15,294

A review of the results of the five-year forecast shows the significant upside potential of the building (*see* Figure 7.10).

Figure 7.10 | Upside Potential

	Current Year $	Year 2 $	Year 3 $	Year 4 $	Year 5 $
NOI	60,936	73,664	79,166	87,284	90,486
CFBT	15,294	28,022	33,524	41,642	44,844

We note the significant increase in the NOI and CFBT in year 2 as a result of bringing an old lease up to market value. There is another increase in revenue in year 4 when tenant D's rent escalates by 10 percent and the operating expenses are reduced because of tax reductions.

Returns on Investments

Office Building Problem Part C—Calculate Cash-on-Cash Return

At the beginning of this problem, you calculated that the present owner had a cash-on-cash return of 12.24 percent at this time. The effects of certain upside events were reflected in the five-year projections.

Now, calculate the cash-on-cash return for the next four years. (Use the CFBT figured previously.) The formula is as follows:

$$\frac{\text{CFBT}}{\text{Initial cash investment}} = \text{Cash-on-cash rate of return}$$

Part C Solution

The initial cash investment is the down payment, which was $125,000 when the current owner bought the building five years ago for $500,000. Utilizing the formula, the cash-on-cash returns for the five-year projection period are as follows:

Current year: $15,294 ÷ $125,000 = 0.1224 (12 percent)
Year 2: $28,022 ÷ $125,000 = 0.2242 (22 percent)
Year 3: $33,524 ÷ $125,000 = 0.2682 (27 percent)
Year 4: $41,642 ÷ $125,000 = 0.3331 (33 percent)
Year 5: $44,844 ÷ $125,000 = 0.3588 (36 percent)

From the owner's position, the return on investment significantly increases from 12 percent to 36 percent over the examined period because of the upside potential. (We can also infer that for the first five years of ownership, the owner did not have a good return on the building and may actually have lost money.) Now, however, it appears that the future return on investment is promising.

The owner's original question to the broker was, What is my building worth? Through this five-year analysis, we have, so far, determined the owner's return on investment currently and projected for the future. However, will a new buyer be interested in the cash-on-cash return of the present owner? Consider that the cash-on-cash return is based on the cash flow before taxes, which is calculated from the present debt service expense and the down payment made by the owner when he bought the building.

Only if the potential owner was assuming the present mortgage and using the same down payment amount would the projected cash-on-cash return be a valid consideration to the investor. This would also mean that the building would be sold for the same price as the purchase price—$500,000. It is rare in commercial transactions that a mortgage is assumed by a buyer. But it is not unusual for a seller to offer to hold a first or second mortgage for a buyer.

Figure 7.11 | Projected Market Values

	Current Year	Year 2	Year 3	Year 4	Year 5
NOI	60,936	73,664	79,166	87,284	90,486
10% CAP					
12% CAP					

Market Value

To truly answer the question, What is my building worth? the building must be viewed from the buyer's point of view: What will an investor pay for the building?

Investors will examine the property and create future projections just as we have done. As noted, they will generally not be concerned with current financing and CFBT. Their focus will be the net operating income. With the NOI and a CAP rate, market value can be determined.

The CAP rate is the investor's desired profit percentage. For purposes of this problem assume the market conditions have investors seeking a 10 percent to 12 percent return on their investments. If we combine the data collected from the seller with the current desired CAP Rates of buyers we can reach some conclusions about the value of the property.

Office Building Problem Part D – Determine Market Value

Fill in the chart in Figure 7.11 with the projected market value for each year at 10 percent and 12 percent CAP rates.

The formula is as follows:

$$\frac{\text{NOI}}{\text{CAP rate}} = \text{Value}$$

A sample calculation for the current year is as follows:

$$\frac{\$60{,}936 \text{ (NOI)}}{0.10 \text{ (CAP rate)}} = \$609{,}360 \text{ (market value)}$$

The solutions are shown in Figure 7.12.

Figure 7.12 | Projected Market Values Solutions

	Current Year	Year 2	Year 3	Year 4	Year 5
NOI	60,936	73,664	79,166	87,284	90,486
10% CAP	609,360	736,640	791,660	872,840	904,860
12% CAP	507,800	613,867	659,717	727,367	754,050

Real Problem

Study the forecast of market values in Figure 7.12. The current owner wants to know the value of the property. You are a commercial REALTOR® who wants to list the building for sale. What do you advise the owner to expect as a sales price? Remember that the building was purchased for $500,000 five years ago and it is now December of the current year.

Part D Solution

This is a judgment call. When an owner asks for advice on the expected sale price, there is no correct answer. However, consider these points:

- What the current owner paid is irrelevant to the next buyer.
- Test the assumptions (projections) for reality.
    - It is December. One might ignore the current year's figures and begin with the year 2 figures. The major rent increase in year 2 is based on replacing an old lease at market value. This is a valid assumption.
    - The other major rent increase is scheduled for year 4 when tenant D's 10 percent rent escalation occurs. Will this tenant still be in the building in three years?
    - Expenses will decrease in year 3 forward as a result of tax reductions.
- How much of the upside potential will the buyer be willing to pay for?

What we have done with our property analysis is known as the **income approach** to valuation. This is typically the method used by bank appraisers to evaluate mortgage applications.

With this problem, if we assume the current year is over and start with year 2 figures as being valid, we might convince a buyer to use the year 3 projections as a basis for their offer.

Based on these numbers and the upside potential, especially with the future tax relief, you might justify telling the owner that his property could sell for $650,000. Perhaps a listing price of $700,000 to allow for negotiations might be appropriate. Because the seller paid $500,000, a sale at $650,000 would probably be agreeable to him.

However, we are only focusing on the income methods of determining market value. Due consideration must be given to the two other methods of evaluation, the **cost approach** and **comparable sales approach**.

The cost approach looks at what is being paid for the building per square foot in comparison to what it would cost to construct the same building today. In this case, the cost per square foot is calculated by dividing the price by the building size, which equals the cost per foot:

$$\$650,000.00 \div 8,700 \text{ SF} = \$74.71 \text{ PSF}$$

Depending on the market area, this price might be a little high for a Class B building. Would someone buy a building if they could build it new at a lower construction cost? For an important location?

Comparative sales are required to complete the evaluation and confirm the projected value. Will the building appraise sufficiently to obtain the desired financing?

These are serious questions, and they require further consideration to answer the client's original question, What is my building worth? However, now you have a detailed analysis and spreadsheets of realistic projections to review with your client.

■ Reality Check: The Buyer's Perspective

There is another important step required to properly estimate the value of this building. The property must be also looked at from the buyer's perspective. Buyers will create their own pro forma, using the information provided by the seller, to determine what they consider the value of a building. The buyer may not agree with the assumptions or projections used by the owner in the operating statements.

Typical items that may be challenged include the following:
- Incorrectly stated facts
    - Lease details—expirations, escalations, renewals, options, or pass-through expenses
- Questionable assumptions
    - Vacancy projections
    - Repair and maintenance projections
- Business style
    - Management—off-site
    - Debt service—leveraging
- Replacement of tenants—projected rent amounts
    - Current market rent

Referring to the assumptions made in the last problem, the buyer might question several items. For example, the buyer might question the projected rent for the lower-level space, which is indicated as immediately rentable at $12 per square foot. How long has the space been vacant? Is it really rentable? For the current year, the lower-level space of 1000 square is projected to be rented for $12 per square foot, or $12,000 annually. The buyer sees a wet basement that "will never be rented! Certainly not at $12."

Vacancy Adjustment Rate—7 percent

The $12,000 projected rent from the basement is, in fact, 8.47 percent of the entire building's current potential rental income of $141,750. The present owner has used 7 percent for vacancy contingency.

The buyer may consider a 10 percent vacancy contingency more realistic.

Repairs and Maintenance Contingency Expense—5 Percent

This is a Class B building, and after the buyer's inspection and engineering report, it is felt that a larger reserve is appropriate. The buyer uses 10 percent in his pro forma.

Figure 7.13 | Investment Pro Forma—Seller's Perspective

(Vacancy—7 percent; repair and maintenance—5 percent; no management)

	Current Yr. $	Year 2 $	Year 3 $	Year 4 $	Year 5 $
Potential rental income	141,750	156,835	160,932	168,013	172,379
Vacancy adjustment	9,923	10,978	11,265	11,791	12,067
Other income	6,000	6,000	6,000	6,000	6,000
Gross operating income	137,827	151,857	155,667	162,252	166,312
Expenses:					
Taxes	50,000	50,000	47,500	45,000	45,000
Repair and maintenance	6,891	7,593	7,783	8,113	8,316
All other expenses	20,000	20,600	21,218	21,885	22,510
Total expenses	76,891	78,193	76,501	74,968	75,826
NOI	60,936	73,664	79,166	87,284	90,486

Business Style

The current owner manages his own building. The buyer hires real estate brokers or property management companies to manage his properties and generally pays them 5 percent of the rent roll as a fee. A management expense is included in the buyer's pro forma.

The percentages mentioned in this section are not uncommon. Many clients target an investment acquisition at 75 percent of NOI, considering 10 percent for vacancy, 10 percent for repair, and 5 percent for management.

To illustrate this concept, compare the two perspectives (Figures 7.13 and 7.14), only changing the percentages used in the assumptions for vacancy and repair and maintenance and adding management expense to the buyer's pro forma.

Figure 7.14 | Investment Pro Forma—Buyer's Perspective

(Vacancy—10 percent; repair and maintenance—10 percent; management—5 percent)

	Current Yr. $	Year 2 $	Year 3 $	Year 4 $	Year 5 $
Potential rental income	141,750	156,835	160,932	168,013	172,379
Vacancy adjustment	14,175	15,683	16,093	16,801	17,237
Other income	6,000	6,000	6,000	6,000	6,000
Gross operating income	133,575	147,152	150,839	157,212	161,142
Expenses:					
Taxes	50,000	50,000	47,500	45,000	45,000
Repair and maintenance	13,357	14,715	15,083	15,721	16,114
Management	6,679	7,358	7,542	7,861	8,057
All other expenses	20,000	20,600	21,218	21,885	22,510
Total expenses	90,036	92,673	91,343	90,436	91,681
NOI	43,539	54,479	59,496	66,776	69,461

Figure 7.15 | Seller's Perspective of Market Value

	Current Year $	Year 2 $	Year 3 $	Year 4 $	Year 5 $
10% CAP	609,360	736,640	791,660	872,840	904,860
12% CAP	507,800	613,867	659,717	727,367	754,050

Quite a Difference!

If the same formulas for determining market value based on NOI and CAP rate are used, the full impact of the different perspectives can be seen. (*See* Figures 7.15 and 7.16.)

As you can see, there is quite a difference in the perceived market values between the property owner and the potential buyer. In our problem, none of the facts changed. Both analyses used the same rent roll information and expenses. What did change were the assumptions: vacancy contingency rate, repair and maintenance percentage, and business style regarding management.

Evaluating Assumptions

Consider these questions when evaluating the assumptions that caused the discrepancies between the two perspectives.

Vacancy Adjustment Rate

- What is the reality?
- How strong is the local market?
- What are the vacancy rates of comparable buildings in the area?
- Is the desired rent competitive?

Repair and Maintenance Percentage

- What is realistic?
- What is the condition and age of the building?
- What does the engineers report say?
- What are the landlord's responsibilities versus the tenant's obligations in the leases?

Management Expenses

- Is it a fair comparison when one party does its own management and the new owner plans to use off-site management?

Figure 7.16 | Buyer's Perspective of Market Value

	Current Year $	Year 2 $	Year 3 $	Year 4 $	Year 5 $
10% CAP	435,000	545,000	595,000	668,000	695,000
12% CAP	363,000	454,000	496,000	556,000	579,000

Commercial Brokerage

In order to do our job properly, we must look at the property from both perspectives (the owner and the potential buyer), validate the facts, and evaluate the assumptions.

Negotiate the assumptions first. If both sides can agree on these variables, and all the other figures are verified, a fair price range can be developed. Within this price range, a deal can be made that is fair to both sides. This is how we do our job.

The previous problem was a typical illustration of the commercial and investment real estate brokerage business. This exercise was designed to show you how some buyers think, how some investors evaluate for negotiating purposes, and that there are no absolutes—just guidelines created by formulas, estimates, and projections.

In a declining value market, as we have seen in recent years, rents may be decreasing, and future years' NOI may be consequently lower than today's. What the building is worth now, may not be what it is worth tomorrow. Spreadsheet analyses show these trends.

Commercial buyers—users—are driven by need: to expand or reduce their business operation. The investment buyer is driven by profit—current income from the property and future upside potential. Both commercial and investment customers will pay for the situation that works for them.

In commercial and investment real estate, we develop lifelong relationships with our customers. As time goes on, their business needs and requirements change, their leases end, or they are ready for another investment. We service our clients over and over again. It is extremely important in all our transactions that everyone be satisfied with the deal and that the buyers and the sellers feel they got a fair deal.

Review Questions

1. As the CAP rate goes up, the value
   a. increases.
   b. decreases.
   c. is not affected.
   d. remains the same.

2. The cash-on-cash return is MOST important to the
   a. seller.
   b. buyer.
   c. bank.
   d. broker.

3. When buying a property, which method of market valuation should be used?
   a. Income approach
   b. Comparable sales
   c. Cost approach
   d. All of these

4. What might buyers question in their pro forma?
   a. Vacancy projections
   b. Contingent repair expenses
   c. Lease details
   d. All of these

5. What expense item is usually based on a percentage?
   a. Taxes
   b. CAM charges
   c. Management fees
   d. Accounting fees

6. Repair and maintenance contingency expense may be determined by
   a. calculating a percentage of the gross operating income.
   b. calculating a percentage of the potential rental income.
   c. using a specific dollar amount.
   d. all of these.

7. In order to sell investment properties, one should first negotiate the
   a. assumptions.
   b. price.
   c. terms.
   d. CAP rate.

8. A spreadsheet shows
   a. future market value.
   b. comparable sales data.
   c. projected income and expenses.
   d. all of these.

9. What effect does leveraging have on an investment?
   a. Always increases the rate of return
   b. Always decreases the rate of return
   c. Reduces the initial investment
   d. Helps sell the property

10. What is the MOST important figure to an investment buyer?
    a. CAP rate
    b. Cash-on-cash return
    c. CFBT
    d. NOI

chapter eight

Depreciation and Cash Flow After Taxes

overview

Suppose we bought an investment property and determined the income, expenses, and net operating income (NOI). Out of the NOI, we paid our partner, the bank, back for the loan. So what do we really get to keep? After subtracting the annual debt service from the NOI, what remains is the cash flow before taxes. Now, the annual income taxes on our property must be calculated and paid. The government give us the ability to reduce those taxes through depreciation. In this chapter, we will explore these topics. ∎

learning objectives

After completing this chapter, you will be able to

- describe depreciation and cost recovery, and
- measure cash flow after taxes.

∎ Key Terms

cash flow after taxes (CFAT)

cost segregation

depreciation (cost recovery)

return on equity

Depreciation or Cost Recovery

In reality, **depreciation** (**cost recovery**) represents the wear and tear on a building over time. As buildings age, certain systems within it become old, and obsolescence begins. An older building may have an electric system with fuses, while a more modern building uses circuit breakers. Roofs, heating systems, and plumbing are all subject to such wear and tear. The exterior and interior structure of the building, grounds, and parking lots all require upgrades and maintenance to counter natural deterioration.

The Internal Revenue Service recognizes such needs and has established rules to allow owners to depreciate their buildings for estimated wear, tear, and obsolescence. Here are some facts on depreciation:

- Depreciation does not apply to the owner's personal residence, but depreciation is required on all commercial and investment property.
- Land does not depreciate.
- Residential-type buildings are depreciated over 27½ years.
- Commercial-type buildings are depreciated over 39 years.
- Capital improvements must also be depreciated.

Land does not depreciate. When a property is purchased, the value of the land and the value of the building must be segregated. Generally, with commercial property purchases, a formal appraisal is conducted and it will include this analysis.

Residential-type buildings include single-family homes (not the owner's personal residence), duplexes, three- or four-family structures, and larger apartment houses.

Commercial-type buildings include offices, retail or industrial spaces, or combinations thereof.

Settlement fees and closing costs may be included in determining the cost basis of the property. Some examples include abstract and title fees, legal fees, title searches, recording fees, surveys, title insurance, transfer taxes, and charges for installing utility services.

Also, any amounts the seller owes that the buyer agrees to pay may be included in the cost basis. These amounts would include back taxes, interest, recording fees, charges for improvements or repairs, and sales commissions.

If you buy a property and assume an existing mortgage, your cost basis will include the amount paid plus the amount of the outstanding mortgage.

Buildings are depreciated using the straight-line depreciation method. This means that the value (cost basis) is divided by 27.5 (residential-type properties) or 39 (commercial-type properties) to determine an equal amount of depreciation allowance each year.

Example:

Depreciation

Small office building—Depreciation schedule 39 years

Purchase price	$495,000
Title search and insurance	1,800
Survey	2,200
Legal fees	1,000
Acquisition cost	$500,000
Less land value	− 110,000
Cost basis	$390,000
Recovery period	÷39 years
Depreciable allowance	$ 10,000

Each year that the building is owned (up to 39 years) the owner may deduct $10,000 from the taxable income of the property for depreciation.

Mixed-use buildings, those containing both residential and commercial units, may have two depreciation schedules. An accountant should be consulted to establish the depreciation schedules for these types of buildings. The general rule, however, is that a building must be 80 percent residential to qualify for the accelerated 27.5 year depreciation schedule.

Leasehold Improvements

Before 2003, the costs of commercial leasehold improvements were depreciated over 39 years. In 2003, the depreciation schedule for certain leasehold improvements was reduced to 15 years. This had been set to expire several times but was extended until the end of 2009. In 2008, this category was expanded to include restaurant buildings and improvements and retail improvements. This reduced cost recovery time schedule for these items actually expired at the end of 2009. However in the Tax Relief, Unemployment Insurance Reauthorization, and Job Creation Act of 2010, the special 15-year cost recovery period for certain leasehold improvements, restaurant buildings, and retail improvements was extended by two years. This was retroactive to January 1, 2010, and expired on December 31, 2011. Unless there is another retroactive extension, leasehold improvements are again being depreciated over 39 years.

Building owners should check with their tax advisor for the current status and treatment of any capital improvements.

Cost Segregation

There are ways to break down the cost components in construction and, with certain improvements, depreciate these costs over different time periods. This is known as **cost segregation**. This will provide shorter depreciation periods for personal property (5 years or 7 years) and for land improvements (15 years), resulting in higher depreciation in the early years of owning the building. Again, tax advisors should be consulted to determine any benefits.

Establishing depreciation schedules should be done with the advice of an accountant or tax advisor.

Cash Flow After Taxes (CFAT)

The annual income from an investment property is subject to income tax. Owners may deduct from that gross income the operating expenses of the property, real estate property taxes, interest on mortgage loans, and depreciation. The remaining net income is taxed at the taxpayer's marginal tax rate. What remains after payment of income taxes is the **cash flow after taxes (CFAT)**, or as it is also called, the after tax cash flow (ATCF).

The cash flow before taxes (CFBT) truly reflects what is left annually from the cash flow of an investment property. From this amount, income taxes must be paid.

Adjustment Required

An additional adjustment to the numbers is required before the tax calculations are made. The operating expense item "repairs and maintenance," which is also called replacement reserve, is a contingent fund of money set aside for emergency repairs. If this money is not spent in a given year, it must be added back to the income before calculating income taxes.

The adjustment would appear as follows:

      Net operating income
+ Repair and maintenance (dollars not spent)
= Adjusted NOI
− Mortgage interest
− Annual depreciation
= Taxable income
× Marginal tax rate
= Income tax

Once the income tax has been calculated, the cash flow after tax may be determined (Figure 8.1). Note: Other deductions may further reduce the taxable income and the property may be eligible for certain tax credits. Always check with an accountant or tax advisor.

Let's look at an example that will tie together many of the concepts previously discussed. We will use the following office building case study:

Potential rental income	$130,000
Less vacancy contingency adjustment	−6,500
Plus other building income	6,000
Equals total operating income	129,500
Less owner's operating expenses	47,475
Equals net operating income (NOI)	$ 82,025

Let us consider that the building is being purchased today for $1,000,000. The property will be financed with a 30 percent down payment ($300,000) with terms on a $700,000 loan at 7 percent interest and a 20-year term.

Figure 8.1 | Cash Flow After Taxes

> Potential rental income
> (Including actual projected and additional rent)
> Less vacancy contingency adjustment
> Plus other building income
> Equals gross operating income
> Less owner's operating expenses
> Equals net operating income (NOI)
> Less annual debt service (when financed)
> Equals cash flow before taxes (CFBT)
> Less income tax
> Equals cash flow after taxes (CFAT)

The annual debt service would be $65,125. The first year's amortization would show that of that total, $16,653 was paid on the principal of the loan and $48,472 was paid on the mortgage interest.

Net operating income (NOI)	$82,025
Less annual debt service (when financed)	− 65,125
Equals cash flow before taxes (CFBT)	$16,900

Next, the income tax must be calculated. To do so, the depreciation must be determined. Note: Land does not depreciate. Assume a land value of 20 percent of the price for this example. With a $1,000,000 sales price, less 20 percent land value ($200,000), the building value is $800,000.

This is an office building, so the depreciation schedule is 39 years; therefore, the depreciation deduction is $20,513 ($800,000 ÷ 39 years).

Remember that in calculating the income tax, if repairs and maintenance was taken as a building expense and, in fact, those monies were not spent that year, then the money must be added back in before the tax is calculated.

The income tax is calculated using the following sequence. (For this example, we will assume the taxpayer is in the 28 percent tax bracket.)

	Net operating income	$82,025
+	Repairs and maintenance	6,475
=	Adjusted NOI	88,500
−	Mortgage interest	− 48,472
−	Annual depreciation	− 20,513
=	Taxable income	19,515
×	Marginal tax rate	0.28
=	Income tax	$5,464

The analysis is concluded as follows:

Net operating income (NOI)	$82,025
Less annual debt service (when financed)	−65,125
Equals cash flow before taxes (CFBT)	16,900
Less income tax	−5,464
Equals cash flow after taxes (CFAT)	$11,436

This is a complete analysis of the property's cash flows, demonstrating current NOI, typical financing, and the impact of depreciation in determining the real return on this investment, after the income taxes have been paid.

The CFAT is also measured as the **return on equity**. Investors will compare various opportunities based on the first year's return on equity. In this case, the following formula applies:

$$\frac{\text{Cash flow after taxes}}{\text{Initial investment}} = \text{Return on equity}$$

$$\frac{\$11,436}{\$300,000} = 3.81 \text{ percent}$$

They may also project forward their return on equity based on appreciation assumptions. They assume that as time goes on, the building will appreciate in value, and that as the mortgage principal is paid down, their equity will increase.

In comparison, if this property were purchased for all cash, no debt service, no mortgage interest deduction, the following would apply:

	Net operating income	$82,025
+	Repair and maintenance	6,475
=	Adjusted NOI	88,500
−	Annual depreciation	−20,513
=	Taxable income	67,987
×	Marginal tax rate	28 percent
=	Income tax	$19,056

Net operating income (NOI)	$82,025
Cash flow before taxes (CFBT)	82,025
(In this case, the CFBT is the NOI.)	
Less income tax	−19,056
Equals cash flow after taxes (CFAT)	$62,969

The return on an all-cash purchase would be referred to as the return on investment (ROI), which is calculated as follows:

$$\frac{\text{Cash flow after taxes}}{\text{Purchase price}} = \text{Return on investment}$$

$$\frac{\$62,696}{\$1,000,000} = 6.30 \text{ percent}$$

Investments show different returns base on several factors, the tax bracket of the owner, and, when financed, the amount of debt and the terms of the loan.

In the previous comparison, the owners may have $1,000,000 to invest. They may buy one building with that money or create several down payments to invest in multiple buildings by leveraging their money. In this case, we would need to examine the cumulative return on all those investments to have a fair comparison. Individual investors may thoroughly examine the numbers right down to their cash flow after taxes and percentage of return on investment based on their specific tax bracket.

Remember that all income tax matters should be reviewed by an accountant or tax advisor.

Review Questions

1. Depreciation is permitted on
   a. land.
   b. office buildings.
   c. your personal residence.
   d. all of these.

2. A retail shopping center would be depreciated over
   a. 27.5 years.
   b. 39 years.
   c. 15 years.
   d. 7 years.

3. Leasehold improvements are currently depreciated over
   a. 7 years.
   b. 15 years.
   c. 27.5 years.
   d. 39 years.

4. Cost segregation provides shorter depreciation periods for
   a. land.
   b. land improvements.
   c. the entire building.
   d. none of these.

5. In determining taxable income, what may be deducted?
   a. Operating expenses
   b. Interest on mortgage loans
   c. Depreciation
   d. All of these

6. In calculating income taxes, unused repair and maintenance funds are
   a. subtracted from the depreciation.
   b. subtracted from the NOI.
   c. added to the NOI.
   d. none of these.

7. Return on equity is determined by dividing the
   a. CFAT by the initial investment.
   b. BTCF by the initial investment.
   c. CFAT by the purchase price.
   d. BTCF by the purchase price.

8. Return on investment is determined by dividing the
   a. CFAT by the initial investment.
   b. BTCF by the initial investment.
   c. CFAT by the purchase price.
   d. BTCF by the purchase price.

9. A small office building is purchased at a cost of $550,000; the land is valued at $82,000. What is the dollar amount of the deduction for depreciation?
   a. $14,000
   b. $17,000
   c. $12,000
   d. Not depreciable

10. If the taxpayer is in the 28 percent tax bracket and the building's taxable income is $47,000, what is the income tax due?
    a. $13,160
    b. $11,750
    c. $33,840
    d. $35,250

chapter nine

Selling Property: Capital Gains Taxes and 1031 Exchanges

overview

Investors have different philosophies about how long they should hold properties. Some buy depressed properties, fix them up, and then sell them in a relatively short period of time. Other investors buy properties and never sell them. Many investors establish a holding period for their investments. Some will typically hold a property for 5, 10, or 15 years and then sell it. Others sell on opportunity.

Whenever an investment property is sold, another level of taxation is triggered: capital gains taxes. Sometimes, people will say, "I cannot sell this property; the capital gains tax would kill me!" What does that really mean? In this chapter, we will explore capital gains taxes and a possible alternative to paying them: a 1031 exchange. ■

learning objectives

After completing this chapter, you will be able to

- describe the capital gains tax on appreciation,
- describe the capital gains tax on depreciation recapture,
- describe the benefits of a 1031 exchange,
- identify the role of the qualified intermediary, and
- describe the rules of exchanges.

Key Terms

1031 exchanges	basis	depreciation recapture tax
adjusted basis	capital gains taxes	

Capital Gains Taxes

Capital gains taxes are taxes on the profit realized from the sale of any capital investment, including real estate.

Short-term capital gains are assets held for less than one year and are taxed at the marginal rate of the taxpayer's income.

Long-term capital gains are assets held for 12 months and sold after May 5, 2003. They are currently taxed at a 15 percent rate, if the taxpayer's marginal tax rate is above the 15 percent income bracket. (Note: In 2008, Congress lowered the tax rate for those in the 15 percent bracket to zero percent. This zero percent tax rate was extended in 2010; however, as of this writing, it is scheduled to expire on December 31, 2012.)

Capital losses occur when an investment or other types of property are sold at a loss. Capital gains can be reduced by capital losses. Net capital losses may be deducted from taxable income up to $3,000 per year, and the unused loss may be carried over to future years.

With commercial and investment properties, there are two capital gains taxes: one on appreciation of value and one on depreciation recapture. Depreciation, which we learned about in the previous chapter, is not permitted to be taken on the owner's personal residence; hence, there is no depreciation recapture tax on the sale of an owner's home.

On commercial and investment properties, there are two capital gains taxes. The first applies to the net gain or profit from the sale and is considered a tax on appreciation of value. The second is a tax on depreciation recapture.

Sale of a Primary/Principal Residence

The profit made from selling a personal residence is subject to a capital gains tax based upon the owner's taxable income level. For most homeowners, this is a tax of 15 percent of its gain in value. However, the IRS offers a residential exclusion, in which homeowners may exclude the first $250,000 in gain ($500,000 if married and filing jointly) on the sale of one home every two years. To be eligible, the homeseller must have owned and resided in the home for two of the past five years before the sale.

Here are two useful terms in calculating capital gains:

- **Basis**—usually the cost of a property
- **Adjusted basis**—the original cost basis plus certain additions and minus certain deductions. An increase in the basis will reduce the taxable gain.

Buyers may add these costs to the basis:

- Title abstracts
- Title insurance
- Attorney fees

Sellers may add these costs to the basis:

- Transfer taxes
- Attorneys fees
- Real estate commissions
- Residential repairs made to the home within 90 days of the sale

In many areas, property values are at a level where the residential exclusion is sufficient to avoid a taxable gain. However, in other areas, property values are high and a sale may be subject to a capital gains tax. Owners in this category should be sure to discuss the sale with their accountant or tax advisor.

Example:

Capital Gains Tax on Sale of Personal Residence

The value of capital improvements made to your home may be added to the purchase price. The resulting adjusted basis and the cost of the sale (i.e., legal fees, real estate commissions, and transfer taxes) are subtracted from the sales price to determine the net profits. Eligible exclusions may then further reduce the taxable net profits.

Purchase price (20 yrs ago)	$125,000
Improvements (added a room)	+ 30,000
Adjusted basis	$155,000
Sale price	$885,000
Less adjusted basis	– 155,000
Less cost of sale	– 56,640
Net profits	$673,360
Capital gain exclusion	– 500,000*
Capital gain	$173,360
Capital gains tax (15%)	**$26,004**

*Married, filing jointly. If this were a single or divorced owner, the exclusion would be $250,000, the gain would be $423,360, and the capital gains tax would be $63,504.

Note: This is a calculation of the federal capital gains tax. Be aware that many states also have a capital gains tax.

Sale of Commercial and investment Property

When it comes to commercial or investment property, almost everyone has heard someone say, "I can't sell my property; the capital gains taxes will kill me!" But what does that really mean? How bad are these taxes?

We previously examined the capital gains taxes on the sale of a personal residence; now, we will examine the effect on commercial and investment properties.

This is how net profits are calculated:

> Contract sale price
> Less adjusted basis
> Less cost of sale
> Equals net profits

Remember these points when calculating capital gains taxes on commercial and investment property:

- This federal tax on net profits was reduced from 20 percent, as of May 5, 2003, to 15 percent. This is considered a tax on appreciation. (If the taxpayer is in the 10 percent or 15 percent tax bracket, the tax is zero.) Note: This rate is in effect through December 31, 2012.
- There is a second tax known as depreciation recapture at a 25 percent tax rate.
- Many states have additional capital gains taxes.

Depreciation Recapture Tax

In a previous chapter, we examined the concept and benefits of depreciation. However, when commercial or investment property is sold, there is a second capital gains tax called the depreciation recapture tax. Depreciation taken on the building and any capital improvements during the ownership period are subject to a recapture tax of 25 percent.

Capital Gains Tax Example: Sale of Commercial Building

A commercial office building was purchased 20 years ago for $125,000. It was improved in stages, with improvements totaling $130,000. Today, it is being sold for $885,000. What are the capital gains taxes?

Step 1—Determine the adjusted basis. This first requires a calculation of depreciation taken to date.

Calculate depreciation on the building:

Purchase price (20 yrs ago)	$125,000
Less land value	– $25,000
Building value	$100,000

Depreciation taken to date on building:

> $100,000 ÷ 39 years = $2,564 per year
> $2,564 × 20 years = $51,282
> Depreciation (39-year schedule) = $51,282

Depreciation must also be taken on capital improvements. Improvements may have been made at various times, creating multiple depreciation schedules.

For this illustration, we will just state the total depreciation to date:

Improvements basis	$130,000
Depreciation taken to date	$35,000

Total depreciation taken:

Building	$51,282
Improvements	$35,000
Total	$86,282

The adjusted basis is determined by adjusting the basis, which is the purchase price, by adding the value of capital improvements made, and subtracting the amount of depreciation taken during the period of ownership.

Calculating adjusted basis:

Purchase price (20 yrs ago)	$125,000
+ Improvements	+130,000
− Depreciation	− 86,282
Adjusted basis	$168,718

Step 2—Calculate the capital gain. The capital gain is determined by subtracting from the sales price the adjusted basis and costs of the sale. What remains are the net profits; this is the capital gain subject to taxation.

Calculating capital gain:

Sale price	$885,000
Less adjusted basis	− 168,718
Less cost of sale	− 56,640
Net profits (capital gain)	$659,642

Step 3—Calculate the capital gains taxes. For tax calculation purposes, the net profits are separated as to the gain from depreciation and the gain from appreciation.

Total capital gains	$659,642
Gain from depreciation	$86,282
Gain from appreciation	$573,360

Depreciation recapture tax (25 percent):

$86,282 × 0.25 = $21,570

Tax on appreciation (15 percent):

$573,360 × 0.15 = $86,004

Federal capital gains tax:

Appreciation	$86,004
Depreciation Recapture	$21,570
Total capital gains tax on a sale of $885,000	**$107,574**

An additional $100,000 tax on the sale of property may pose a problem for most investors. However, there is a way to defer the capital gains taxes by doing a 1031 tax-deferred exchange.

■ 1031 Exchanges

The Revenue Act of 1918 was the first income tax code in the United States. It did not address exchanges. In 1921, the code was modified and included the first definitions of tax-deferred exchanges. In 1935, the foundations of the current statutes were established, including defining the qualified intermediary. At that time, the statute was known as section 112 of the tax code.

In 1954, the statute was changed to section 1031, and most of present-day exchange rules were defined. Various modifications and clarifications have occurred since. The most significant change, in 2002, allowed tenants-in-common (TICs), who have co-ownership of properties, to be used in 1031 exchanges.

A **1031 exchange** allows the seller of real estate to defer the capital gains taxes on that sale (the relinquished property) by buying another real estate property (the replacement property).

There are many rules and requirements for exchanges. The IRS requires that the taxpayer have an independent third party conduct the exchange. This person is generally referred to as the qualified intermediary (QI) or accommodator.

IRS rules prohibits any attorney, accountant or real estate agent the property owner has worked with within the last two years from serving as the Qualified Intermediary.

Exchanges are considered federal in nature because properties in one state can be exchanged for properties in another. Consequently, there are no licensing requirements for qualified intermediaries. (But owners should always check with their state; requirements may change.)

Unfortunately, this lack of licensure requirements has led to some criminal activity on the part of some unscrupulous QIs. Many title companies and some banks have gone into the 1031 exchange business and offer this service. Independent practitioners should be questioned about their fiduciary policies. Ask whether they offer bonded, insurance guarantees so the money is protected.

The way an exchange generally works is that the taxpayer will relinquish the property title (of the property being sold) to the qualified intermediary, who will actually sell the property and hold the sale proceeds. Then, the QI will act as the buyer of the replacement property being purchased. The QI prepares all the required documentation, provides complete accounting to the taxpayer, and concludes by transferring the title of the newly acquired property to the taxpayer.

Qualified Properties

Replacement property acquired in an exchange must be of like kind to the property being relinquished. The term *like kind* means similar in nature or character, notwithstanding differences in grade or quality. Both the relinquished and the replacement properties must be held by the exchanger for investment purposes or for productive use in their trade or business. Personal residences and personal property are not eligible for exchange.

General Rules for Determining Qualified Properties

The rules for determining qualified properties are as follows:

- Identify the replacement property within 45 days after transfer of the relinquished property.
- Receive title to the replacement property within 180 days after the transfer of the relinquished property.
- All proceeds of the sale of the relinquished property must be held by a third party, a qualified intermediary.
- All cash proceeds must be invested to fully defer taxable gain.

There are three acquisition rules:

- The three-investment property rule states that the exchanger must identify up to—but no more than—three potential investment properties during the acquisition period.
- The 100 percent rule dictates that, in the event that three or more like-kind investment properties are selected as replacement investment properties, the aggregate market value of said investment properties may not exceed 200 percent of the market value of relinquished investment property.
- The 95 percent exception applies if the exchanger identifies more than three properties that are worth more than 200 percent of the value of all relinquished properties. If that's the case, then the exchanger must acquire 95 percent of the value of all properties identified.

Full and Partial Exchanges

If all the proceeds of the sale are used to purchase a replacement property and the value, equity, and debt are all equal to or greater than the original property, then a full deferral of the capital gains tax is possible. If all these rules are not complied with, a partial deferral of the taxes may be possible.

The term *boot* is used to describe other nonqualified property received in an exchange that is not like kind to the property acquired. (For example: cash, stock, personal property). The boot proceeds in the exchange are considered a gain and are taxable.

The IRS requires that the taxpayer be "arms distant" from the 1031 exchange. A qualified intermediary should be consulted.

Example 1:

Full Deferral of Capital Gains Tax	Relinquished Sold Property	Replacement Purchased
Value	$450,000	$600,000
Equity	$200,000	$200,000
Debt	$250,000	$400,000

A property valued at $450,000 was sold, and a property valued at $600,000 was purchased. The equity in the property being sold was used as the down payment on the purchase. A higher mortgage was obtained. In this case, each category is "equal to or greater than."

Example 2:

Partial Deferral of Capital Gains Tax	Relinquished Sold Property	Replacement Purchased
Value	$450,000	$600,000
Equity	$200,000	**$150,000**
Debt	$250,000	$450,000

In this case, the value and debt increased, but the equity was reduced (not equal to or greater than). On the sale, the taxpayer took $50,000 from the equity for other purposes, **thereby creating cash boot of $50,000**, which is subject to the capital gains tax.

Example 3:

Partial Deferral of Capital Gains Tax	Relinquished Sold Property	Replacement Purchased
Value	$450,000	$350,000
Equity	$200,000	$200,000
Debt	$250,000	**$150,000**

In this example, the property being purchased cost less than the property being sold. The equity in the property being sold was used for the down payment, reducing the amount of financing required. **This created mortgage boot of $100,000**, which is subject to capital gains tax.

Review Questions

1. Capital gains taxes are applicable to
   a. commercial buildings.
   b. the investor's personal residence.
   c. investment properties.
   d. all of these.

2. The sale of an investor's personal residence
   a. is not subject to capital gains taxes.
   b. may allow an exclusion of $250,000 for single taxpayers.
   c. is taxable at 25 percent of gain.
   d. none of these.

3. The depreciation recapture tax is
   a. 10 percent.
   b. 15 percent.
   c. 20 percent.
   d. 25 percent.

4. On appreciation of a commercial building, taxpayers in the 28 percent tax bracket must pay a capital gains tax of
   a. 10 percent.
   b. 15 percent.
   c. 20 percent.
   d. 25 percent.

5. A qualified intermediary is licensed by
   a. the federal government.
   b. the state government.
   c. the local county government.
   d. none of these.

6. A 1031 exchange _____ capital gains taxes.
   a. eliminates
   b. reduces
   c. increases
   d. defers

7. Who may NOT serve as a qualified intermediary if they have done business with the taxpayer in the last two years?
   a. Accountants
   b. Attorneys
   c. Real estate agents
   d. All of these

8. For a full deferral of capital gains taxes, what must be "equal to or greater than"?
   a. Value
   b. Equity
   c. Debt
   d. All of these

9. In order to do a 1031 exchange, the new property must be acquired within ___ days from the start of the exchange transaction.
   a. 45
   b. 60
   c. 180
   d. 360

10. In a 1031 exchange, the replacement property must be declared within _____ days after transfer of the relinquished property.
    a. 45
    b. 60
    c. 90
    d. 180

chapter ten

Dealing with Other Brokers

overview

In commercial real estate, a significant amount of the inventory consists of open, nonexclusive listings. Thus, a large portion of the business is done in cooperation with other brokers. This necessitates establishing relationships with agents from other firms. In addition, a separate series of forms and agreements is used when working with other brokers. ■

learning objectives

After completing this chapter, you will be able to

- describe referral agreements,
- describe how to structure co-brokerage agreements,
- recognize the value of using non-circumvention agreements, and
- relate the importance of showing records.

■ Key Terms

| co-broke agreement | Noncircumvention and Nondisclosure Agreement | notice of showing |

Commission Splits

Commercial practitioners look upon splitting commissions with other brokers from a fairness point of view—one should be paid for what they do. Market conditions will also affect the splits offered other brokers, as will their listing agreements with property owners.

In a market where there is no inventory (i.e., very few properties are for sale or lease), listing a property may be considered a tremendous achievement that required a lot of work. Other brokers in the area understand this and, in general, acknowledge that the listing broker deserves a larger commission than the selling broker. In contrast, when interest rates are very high and there are very few buyers and a tremendous amount of inventory, listings are considered less valuable than qualified buyers. Commission splits between brokers at those times favor the selling side.

In other markets, splits rarely fluctuate, and in many of those areas, equal value is given to both sides of the transaction—brokers split commissions on a 50/50 basis. The splits between brokers are negotiable and may be affected by local conditions or the overall economy.

Commission Overrides

The listing agreements obtained from property owners sometimes provide for an override commission. This, in essence, allows the listing broker to market the property to other brokers offering a full commission. This added incentive to the brokerage community helps promote the property.

Referral Agreements

Referral agreements are made within the trade when a residential agent brings a customer to a commercial agent. These situations usually result in the commercial agent servicing or "running" the customer (doing all the work). If a deal results, the referring agent earns a referral fee based on the commission the commercial agent receives. Examine the sample agreement in Figure 10.1.

The way the referral will be calculated and by whom it will be paid must be clarified. Several situations can occur.

Typically, referring agents will either have a customer representing the buying or leasing side or will have a client who has a property to list for sale or lease. They are entitled to a referral fee based on that side of the transaction only. In fact, the commercial practitioner receiving the referral may need to co-broke with another commercial broker to make a deal.

Sometimes, getting the referral requires that a more significant portion of the commission be paid for the fee. If this occurs, the referring agent usually has control of a "hot" property. This agreement may be structured to pay a referral fee "off the top"—a percentage of the total commission involved. Brokers entering into such an agreement would then have to disclose the referral fee due to any other broker who may wish to share the listing or be prepared to absorb the expense of the referring fee entirely for the commission they will receive.

Figure 10.1 | Sample Referral Agreement

REFERRAL AGREEMENT—on stationery
(Sample)

Referring agent: _____
Agent's company: _____

Office: _____
Phone: _____ Fax: _____ E-mail: _____

Name of referral: _____
Referral company: _____

Address: _____
Phone: _____ Fax: _____ E-mail: _____

Client's requirements:
_____
_____

The real estate commission will be split:

	From the
_____% to (your company)	_____ Listing side
_____% to (referring company)	_____ Buying or leasing side of the transaction

Remarks:
_____
_____

Acknowledgment

Referral fee agreed to by:

_____   Date: _____
Broker (your company)

_____   Date: _____
Broker (referring company)

Some brokers allow their agents to enter in referral agreements with other agents with the understanding that any fees paid will be out of the agent's, not the broker's, share of the commissions.

These points must all be clarified and appropriately recorded. The sample referral agreement in Figure 10.1 illustrates content and format. Check local and state laws as to any requirements or regulations in using such a form.

Co-Broke Agreements

Considerable real estate brokerage business is done with one firm representing the selling, or landlord, side of the transaction and another firm representing the buyer or tenant. This scenario necessitates written agreements between all the brokers involved.

When a commercial practitioner has an exclusive agreement for sale or lease of a property and wants to share the listing with another broker, a **co-broke agreement** is used. Such an agreement identifies the property and the rules under which the listing is shared, including commission rates, commission splits, registration of customers, and other conditions. These forms are usually printed in advance in a fill-in-the-blanks format. Most commercial real estate companies have their own forms. A sample is provided in Figure 10.2.

Figure 10.2 | Sample Co-Brokerage Agreement

CO-BROKERAGE AGREEMENT—on stationery
(Sample)

This Broker Cooperation Agreement is made this _____ day of _____ 20_____, by and between:
_____ (Name and Address of Listing Broker) _____ hereinafter referred to as the LISTING BROKER and _____ (Name and Address of Selling Broker) _____ hereinafter referred to as the SELLING BROKER.

Subject Property: _____
_____

LISTING BROKER has listed the above subject property for sale, lease, or exchange and agrees to cooperate with SELLING BROKER under the following conditions:

1. SELLING BROKER must introduce the customer to an authorized representative of LISTING BROKER and promptly confirm in writing the date of the inspection and complete identity of the prospect.

2. SELLING BROKER must be authorized to submit a proposal on behalf of the prospect and must do so in writing, outlining all the terms and conditions of the offer.

3. SELLING BROKER agrees that LISTING BROKER will negotiate any offers with the property owner and be present for the submission of any offers on the subject property.

4. LISTING BROKER hereby agrees to share the commission, as earned and received from the property owner, for a competed sale, lease, or exchange of the subject property on a 50-50 basis with SELLING BROKER. Commissions due SELLING BROKER are subject to any of the listing conditions including the rate and manner of payment of the commission for particular offerings imposed by principals or agreed to by this company. Before any commission is deemed earned, a Co-Brokerage Agreement must be executed between this office and the cooperating broker.

Agreed and Accepted:

_____   _____
SELLING BROKER   LISTING BROKER

A co-brokerage agreement gives the listing broker control of the relationship. It establishes the way the listing broker wants to do business. Note these important points:

- The ability of the listing broker to register potential customers with the owner is established in condition 1 by requiring the cooperating broker to identify the name of the prospect.
- Condition 2 establishes that any offers must be in writing and that if the selling broker is submitting an offer on behalf of the customer, the selling broker has authority to do so.
- The listing broker is in control of any negotiations. However, per condition 3, the selling broker may be present when offers are presented.
- Commission splits between the brokers are established in condition 4. (Note: A 50-50 split is used in the sample for illustrative purposes only. All commission splits between the brokers are negotiable.) Further, the selling broker agrees to be bound by any commission rates or manner of payment imposed by the owner and agreed to by the listing broker.

As with the other sample forms presented in this book, check local laws and make any appropriate changes before using the samples.

Some co-brokerage agreements may cover many other points and situations that might be necessary for more complex properties or larger transactions. Other national firms may also have their own standard forms for this purpose. It is typical for the listing broker to create or issue the co-brokerage agreement.

Co-Brokering Open Nonexclusive Listings

It has been established that a considerable portion of a commercial practitioner's listing may be direct from the owner but nonexclusive. Sometimes, these properties will be promoted by the listing broker in advertisements or on commercial listing services (perhaps generically with a basic description of the property but no specific address), or the broker may have permission for a sign on the property. Or even if the listing is not being promoted, one broker calls another broker, asking whether that broker has a property that would fit her customer's requirement. How does this broker handle cooperating with the other broker (whom he may not know), while protecting himself and the listing?

Let us also consider the possibility that the other broker introduces the property to the customer and then that customer goes directly to the owner, circumventing both brokers. Two different agreements are available to help with these circumstances, but caution and common sense must prevail. Immediate registration of all potential prospects with the property owner is the best form of protection.

The first form, the Broker Cooperation Agreement (see Figure 10.3), is very similar to the Co-Brokerage Agreement. It employs a two-step process. The known generic description is inserted first; then the cooperating broker signs the agreement. Upon receipt of the signed Brokerage Cooperation Agreement, the listing broker sends full details and the address of the property.

The second method used in co-brokering open nonexclusive listings is known as a **Non-Circumvention and Nondisclosure Agreement**. This use of this agreement, or a modification of it, may also be requested by property owners, no matter what type of listing is given (open or exclusive).

Figure 10.3 | Broker Cooperation Agreement

BROKER COOPERATION AGREEMENT—on stationery

(Sample)

This Broker Cooperation Agreement is made this _____ day of _____ 20_____, by and between: _____ (Name and Address of Listing Broker) _____ hereinafter referred to as the LISTING BROKER and _____ (Name and Address of Selling Broker) _____ hereinafter referred to as the SELLING BROKER.

LISTING BROKER has listed the below subject property for sale, lease, or exchange and agrees to cooperate with SELLING BROKER under the following conditions:

1. SELLING BROKER must introduce the customer to an authorized representative of the LISTING BROKER and promptly confirm in writing the date of the inspection and complete identity of the prospect.

2. SELLING BROKER must be authorized to submit a proposal on behalf of the prospect and must do so in writing, outlining all the terms and conditions of the offer.

3. SELLING BROKER agrees that LISTING BROKER will negotiate any offers with the property owner and be present for the submission of any offers on the subject property.

4. LISTING BROKER hereby agrees to share the commission, as earned and received from the property owner, for a competed sale, lease, or exchange of the subject property on a 50-50 basis with SELLING BROKER. Commissions due SELLING BROKER are subject to any of the listing conditions including the rate and manner of payment of the commission for particular offerings imposed by principals or agreed to by this company. Before any commission is deemed earned, a Co-Brokerage Agreement must be executed between this office and the cooperating broker.

5. Subject property is initially described as follows: _____
_____
_____
_____

Upon acceptance and signature of this agreement by SELLING BROKER, LISTING BROKER will insert or attach a complete description and detailed location of the subject property, sign this agreement, and return a copy to SELLING BROKER.

These terms are agreed as stated:
SELLING BROKER

_____
Authorized Signature
Print Name Below

_____

Communication Information:
Phone: _____ Fax: _____ E-mail: _____

You are herby authorized to offer this property to your customers.
LISTING BROKER

_____
Authorized Signature
Detailed subject property description: _____
_____

The Noncircumvention and Nondisclosure Agreement is primarily addressed to the customer, buyer, or tenant, indicating that information about the property is proprietary. The information the customer will receive about the property is confidential and may not be shared with other parties with the exception of partners, directors, key employees, or related parties (i.e., attorney or accountant) on a need-to-know basis.

Properties are sometimes technically not on the market, but after being approached, the owners may agree to consider a purchase by a certain party. However, they do not want the word to get out that they are for sale. In such cases, a confidentiality agreement is required. If word of a pending sale gets out, the owner risks loss of business or employees.

Sale of investment properties requires disclosure of tenants' lease information, profits, expenses, losses, and other sensitive information. Owners may not want such information made public and may require a Noncircumvention and Nondisclosure Agreement (*see* Figure 10.4 for a sample).

Commercial practitioners can utilize such an agreement to help protect owner's information and indirectly their commissions. Because the format addresses the customer, the customer subscribes to the conditions and signs it. The agreement is also signed by all the brokers involved—the broker representing the owner (you as the listing broker) and the broker(s) representing the customer; the brokers and the principals are bound to the same confidentiality. The agreement states that no party will contact the owner without the written permission of the owner's agent (you). Execution of this agreement requires disclosure of the customer, who may now be registered with the owner, protecting all brokers involved from circumvention.

The Noncircumvention and Nondisclosure Agreement is one of the strongest documents available to help brokers prevent others from going around them and trying to defraud them of their commissions. General agreements of this type can be developed for use in one's office under the guidance of an attorney and giving due consideration to state and local laws. The sample viewed is for a purchase. Other agreements are specifically for leases or other transactions.

However, care should be taken in using these agreements. Many properties will require a specific agreement drafted to the conditions regarding that particular building or property. These are often complicated agreements and should be created by an attorney. If involved with a listing where you are asked to sign a confidentiality agreement or a Noncircumvention and Nondisclosure Agreement, be sure to have it reviewed by your attorney before signing it.

■ Showing Records and Activity Reports

A commercial property sale can often take a considerable period. Successful business owners are often short on patience—they expect immediate action or results. These two points can obviously conflict. The solution is communication.

With commercial and investment clients, you have opportunities for repeat business as the needs of their businesses change. Properly handled, these customers can literally be clients for life. The key to future brokerage business is periodic and regular communication.

Figure 10.4 | Sample Noncircumvention and Nondisclosure Agreement

As a consideration moving the parties to a Certain Agreement to be made between the undersigned Seller, Lessor, Assignor or Listing Broker, (hereinafter referred to as "Seller") and Purchaser, Lessee, and any Consultant or Broker on the Purchaser's behalf (hereinafter referred to as "Purchaser") for any property owned or leased directly by the Seller before the signing of any contract and as a condition precedent to the consummation of all prior negotiations and to the creation of any contract and each and every term thereof, the undersigned parties do hereby covenant and agree to the following:

1. None of the materials furnished to the Purchaser by the Seller will be used or duplicated by the Purchaser in any way detrimental to Seller or for any purpose other than evaluating a possible purchase, or lease, of the property described therein. Therefore, the undersigned agrees to keep all Confidential Information (other than information which is a matter of public record or is provided in other sources readily available to the public) strictly confidential; provided, however, that the Confidential Information may be disclosed by Purchaser to directors, officers and employees of the undersigned, but only to these individuals. and to a prospective Purchaser's outside counsel and accounting firm (all of whom are collectively referred to as "related parties") who in Purchaser's considered judgment need to know such information for the purpose of evaluating a possible purchase or lease of the property by Purchaser. The undersigned party will promptly, upon the request of the Seller, deliver to the Seller all Confidential Information furnished to them by the Seller or the Listing Broker, whether furnished before or after the date of this letter.

2. The undersigned agrees not to make any of the Confidential Information available, or disclose any of the contents of confidential information, or either the fact that discussions or negotiations are taking place concerning a possible sale, lease or assignment of any property to Purchaser or any of the terms, covenants, conditions, or other facts with respect to any such transaction, including status thereof, to any other person other than as permitted by the preceding paragraph unless such person, or entity has been identified in writing to the Seller; the Seller has approved in writing the disclosure of the Confidential Information to such person; and such person has entered into a written confidentiality Agreement with the Seller.

3. The undersigned will direct all parties to whom Confidential information is made available not to make similar disclosures. Any such disclosure shall be deemed made by, and be the responsibility of, the undersigned.

4. The undersigned agree that the spirit of this Agreement is one of mutual trust and confidence between the undersigned parties and the reliance upon the undersigned to co what is fair and equitable in their business relationship to each other, and it is further agreed to this Agreement that no effort will be made to circumvent the letter and spirit of this Agreement in an effort to contact the Seller to avoid/gain the commission, fee or other forms of consideration which assures to the benefit of one, or more, on the undersigned parties to the exclusion of any of the other parties.

Figure 10.4 | Sample Noncircumvention and Nondisclosure Agreement (continued)

Non-Circumvention & Non-Disclosure Agreement Page 2 of 2

5. It is agreed by the undersigned parties not to contact, or attempt to contact, the other party bring represented , nor to directly contact the Seller/Purchaser, as applicable, without the written approval from the undersigned party representing the Seller/Purchaser, as applicable.

6. This agreement shall be considered to include the Corporation(s), Company(s), Partnership(s), Syndicate(s), Division(s), Employees, Consultants, business contacts, assignees, family and heirs of each of the undersigned.

7. It is agreed that any controversy, or claim arising out of, or relating to this Agreement, or the breach thereof, which is not settled between the undersigned parties, shall be settled by arbitration in accordance with the rules of the American Arbitration Association, with hearings to take place in _____ State, at a time and place mutually agreed upon, or finally set by the assigned arbitrator. Any judgments rendered by the Arbitrator may be entered in any Court having jurisdiction over the parties and subject matter of the controversy, and shall include any reward to the aggrieved party so long as the award relates to the total remuneration to be received as a result of the business conducted between the parties pursuant to this Agreement and should include all court costs, and attorney's fees equal to twenty-five percent (25%) of the award, and any other costs or damages reasonable necessary to adjudicate, and said award shall be not less than fifty percent (50%) of the commissions, fees, remuneration and other considerations due and payable as a result of the disputed transactions.

8. This agreement shall be governed by, and construed in accordance with, the laws of the State of _____.

9. This Agreement may only be changed by a written notice signed by all parties, and may not be changed orally.

ACCEPTED

"Purchaser"   "Seller" – Listing Broker

By: _____   By: _____
_____
  (Print Name and Title)
                                                               Agreed this ____ day of _____ 20__
Broker or Consultant for "Purchaser"

By: _____

Firm: _____

This is most important when you have a current assignment from one of your clients. The client needs to know you are working on the project, marketing and showing the property to potential buyers or tenants. You may be working very hard, but if you don't communicate this, the client may think you are doing nothing and give the listing to another broker.

One also needs to register all potential customers with the property owner as soon as possible. This way, if one of the customers contacts the owner directly, the owner will know it is due to your introducing that customer to the property and that you will expect to be recognized as the broker if they come to a sale or lease agreement.

At least once a month (preferably once a week), a written report should be sent to each property owner you represent stating the marketing activity on the property. Certain properties and owners may need more frequent communication. It is important that these records be in writing. All customers and other brokers who have been shown the property should be listed. This is especially important with a nonexclusive listing, in which a customer (or another unscrupulous broker) could try to bypass you. Entries might take the following form:

- 2/15/13—Showing: Mr. John Jones, Advanced Advertising Corp.
- 2/17/13—Inspection: Ms. Judy Jacobs, Main Street Realty
- 2/18/13—Showing: Mr. Frank Brown, Ace Insurance (Represented by Mrs. Mary Smith, Smith Commercial Real Estate)

Note that the list includes not only identification of customers and broker inspections, in a co-broking arrangement but also identifies both the broker and the broker's customer. It is important that the rules in co-broke agreements be enforced. Other brokers must disclose the names of their customers so the listing broker can register them with the property owners.

Activity reports may show a pattern. When making reports, show the good and the bad. If several customers went to the property and were put off by the condition, share this information with the owners and urge them to clean it up. When the property has been shown to a number of prospects and all declined to make an offer, it is probably overpriced. This information might influence the owner to lower the price.

Showing Record Master File System

Various offices conduct brokerage business in many different ways. In some offices, when a new listing is taken, all the agents get together for a general inspection (this is a good idea). Many offices have an "up" system, whereby new customer inquiries are divided equally among the agents in one manner or another. In some offices, there is a specialized division for each type of commercial property. It is not always possible for the listing agent to accompany every inspection or showing of the property.

What is suggested is a central file for each listed property and the creation of a simple in-house notice of showing form. Each time someone shows the property or introduces it to another broker, the form is completed and filed in this central file. In this manner, when the listing person wants to report activity to the owner, the showing records are available in the file. This is especially useful when the owner calls unexpectedly and asks about activity on the listing. The agent can locate the file quickly and provide a report. Such a form may be very simple, as the sample depicted in Figure 10.5. The purpose of this form is simply for office record keeping.

Figure 10.5 | Sample Showing Record

SHOWING RECORD
(Sample)

Property shown: _____

Listing # _____

Date of showing: _____

Name of customer: _____

Customer's company: _____

Showing agent: _____

If co-broke, firm name: _____

Co-broke agent: _____

Notice of Showing

In addition to the monthly summary, an instant **notice of showing**, to immediately register a customer or another broker introduced to a property, may be prudent. This is done with two purposes: to protect the broker and to show the client your work. This needs to be done in writing so that a permanent record is established.

With modern business tools, it would seem feasible to provide these notifications electronically via e-mail. If you register customers by e-mail, be sure to store that e-mail in your files. Depending on the size and scope of the project, a letter serving as a notice of showing for each prospect may be more appropriate.

You may also create a standard notice of showing form for use within your firm. The format for such a letter or form is shown in Figure 10.6. This is an essential step because showing records presents the work the broker is doing and registers potential prospects to help protect commissions.

Figure 10.6 | Notice of Showing

Indicate your name, company, and contact information.

Address of the building owner and date.

NOTICE OF SHOWING

We have presented your property located at _____ to _____ (company name of buyer or tenant), represented by _____ (individual's name and title or name of cooperating broker and name of the broker's customer).

We will advise you of their level of interest. If the above party contacts you directly, please notify us and direct them to speak to us as your agent.

Thank you,

Review Questions

1. Which condition might affect commission splits between brokers?
   a. General economy
   b. Supply and demand of properties
   c. Negotiations between brokers
   d. All of these

2. When a listing broker is able to offer another broker a full commission, it is called
   a. a bonus commission.
   b. a premium program.
   c. an override commission.
   d. an incentive program.

3. "Running" the customer means
   a. referring a customer to another broker.
   b. doing all the work.
   c. showing a specific property.
   d. e-mailing property descriptions.

4. Referral fees may be paid based on
   a. the listing or selling side of the transaction.
   b. the entire commission.
   c. just the agents commission.
   d. all of these.

5. Co-brokerage agreements are controlled by the
   a. listing agent.
   b. selling agent.
   c. property owner.
   d. buyer or tenant.

6. Co-brokerage agreements usually require
   a. the customer's signature.
   b. all offers to be telephonic.
   c. selling brokers to be bound by any commission terms imposed by the owner.
   d. offers to be presented by the selling broker.

7. What is the *BEST* way broker can protect their potential commissions?
   a. Only taking exclusive listings
   b. Having written co-broke agreements with other brokers
   c. Immediate registration of all potential prospects with the property owner
   d. Using open confirmation letters

8. What is the main advantage to the broker in using the Noncircumvention and Nondisclosure Agreement?
   a. Guarantees the commission rate
   b. The potential customer and all brokers sign the agreement
   c. It keeps details of the listing confidential
   d. It serves as an exclusive listing agreement

9. What is the *MOST* important reason to use a notice of showing form?
   a. Are good communication tools
   b. Easy to keep as a permanent records
   c. To show activity to owners
   d. To keep brokers honest

10. Registering customers with owners should be done
    a. by e-mail.
    b. by written notice.
    c. only by a monthly report.
    d. only when requested.

chapter eleven

Marketing for Success

overview

Previous chapters examined various forms and agreements used in commercial real estate, the so-called tools of the trade you need to conduct your business. But more than just paperwork, real estate is a people business. To succeed one needs to market products, services, and—just as importantly—oneself.

As a student of commercial and investment real estate, there is much to learn about marketing. Remember this somewhat corny phrase "if it is to be, it is up to me." Success requires a marketing plan, plenty of prospecting, and consistent efforts. ■

learning objectives

After completing this chapter, you will be able to

- recognize the most effective ways of promoting property,
- describe the benefits of using the internet as a marketing tool, and
- describe how to create a marketing plan.

■ Key Term

QR code

The Internet

Today's real estate customer will first go to the Internet to search for information about properties and the markets in which they are located. Only when they find something of interest will they investigate further. This may involve calling the listing agent or owner or driving the area to see what it is like and what other businesses are in the neighborhood. While our primary marketing efforts must be Web-orientated, traditional methods of marketing are also important, and we will discuss these first.

Traditional Forms of Advertising

Signs

One of the most effective advertisements for a commercial property is still a sign on the building. Most business owners will travel to the locations to which they are considering expanding or moving their business. They will look for buildings or sites that support their purposes. Often, these people will not be completely familiar with the area and will seek brokers to work with. Noting that a certain brokerage firm has several signs in the desired area may prompt them to contact that broker for assistance.

It is important to know what other buildings and properties are available in the close proximity to those where you have a sign posted. When you place a sign on a building, prepare to talk about other available properties in that area. A customer may like the area but not the specific building. Know your competition and what buildings are listed by other brokers near the property where you have your sign; establish a co-broke arrangement so you will be able to show those properties as well. Perhaps, you will only make "half a deal." But if you don't, the prospect might call your competitors directly and you would lose the opportunity to service the customer.

Signs are so important to brokers that typical listing agreements will include a sentence stating the following: "Owner grants permission to broker to post a sign on the property." These agreements tell the owners that this is an expected, routine, and necessary tool in properly promoting their property.

There are, however, exceptions where the broker is best served in striking that sentence from the agreement before presenting it to an owner. For example, you may have a client who wants you to sell a building that is currently used as a bowling alley. What would happen to the bowling leagues if a For Sale sign appeared on the building? They might go elsewhere and the owner would lose the business. A similar situation might exist with the sale of a small medical building. Patients who fear that their doctor is leaving the area might seek another physician.

Print Media

Depending on your market area, print media may be very effective or hardly useful at all.

The four key types of print advertising are as follows:

- Local newspapers may be very effective for smaller local properties.
- Regional newspapers are attractive to clients searching for larger properties and to investors.

- Ethnic newspapers, often in languages other than English, are located in areas with strong ethnic populations. If the property is in such an area, or if your office services a community, these papers may be valuable advertising tools. Commercial markets, especially for large projects and investment properties, are international. Advertising in other countries may also be effective.
- Trade papers include publications (newspaper and magazines) that are directed to the real estate industry. Property owners, customers, and other brokers read these, and they are very effective in marketing properties. In addition, other industries have their own publications too. You might consider marketing an office building in the local or regional law journal or insurance brokers' magazine. Check the reference section of your library for some ideas.

Classified Advertising

The purpose of a classified ad is to make the phone ring. An ad should provide enough information to get attention and raise curiosity. Ads do not sell or lease properties—sale agents do. Your ads should include basic information but never more than a clue as to where the property is located. Supposed you have an exclusive and you publish the property address. A potential customer drives by the building, likes the area but not the building, sees your competitor's sign on another building, calls the competitor, and makes the deal. In contrast, if they had to call you about your ad, you would have the opportunity to make an appointment with the customer to show your building. With your market knowledge, you could also discuss other available buildings.

Ads might include the name of the town or locational phrases such as "South Shore" or "Industrial Park Setting." The ad might include the size of the unit, the type (store, warehouse, industrial, etc.), the cost per month, and important features such as traffic counts and ceiling height. Make the ad a teaser so the reader has to call you for details. Once you get them on the phone, it's up to you.

Press Releases—You Are the News

Publications, especially trade publications, write about activity in the marketplace. People want to know what buildings have been sold, to whom, and for how much. When you complete a sale or lease transaction, create a press release of all the facts and send it to your local papers and trade publications. You might just be the next front page article. Readers of trade papers might think that if you can do that for one party, then you can do it for them too!

Commercial Flyers

Flyers can be designed to promote properties to customers, other brokers, or both. They can be printed, mailed or faxed, or created electronically and e-mailed.

Flyers are a communication tool to an audience that is interested in a specific type of building. All flyers should include the size of the space available, the entire building size, the property size, and a picture. Sometimes a picture of the interior can tell a better story than an exterior photograph of the building. For example, when selling a restaurant, a picture of the dining room with tables set might create a strong impression. For large properties, aerial photos may be appropriate.

Pricing information on the flyer must include any additional rent items (e.g., CAM charges, electric or utilities fees paid by the tenant). Other features that should be highlighted for various property types include the following:

- Retail stores
    - Demographic information, population, and medium income
    - Traffic count
    - Tenant mix, anchor store, and/or other tenants in the immediate area
    - Free-standing or number of stores in center
    - Note if in-line or end-cap position
- Industrial buildings
    - Ceiling height
    - Number of overhead doors, loading docks, and tail-boards
    - Column placements
    - Floor loads
    - Amperage
    - Type of sprinklers
- Office buildings
    - Class
    - High-tech features
    - Parking; spaces for employees, visitors
    - Security
    - View; how many stories, on what floor is available space
    - Floor plan (layout)
- Investment properties
    - Number of rental units
    - Vacancy percentage
    - Net operating income (NOI)
    - Capitalization rate (CAP Rate)
    - For retail or office names of major tenants

Subleases will typically be rented "as is," so it is important that a detailed floor plan be included in those flyers.

Broker Open Houses

A good way to expose a new listing to other brokers is with a broker open house. Invite all commercial brokers in the area to an inspection of the property. These events are fairly common for office and industrial buildings. The term *open houses* is generally thought of as a residential marketing tool; with commercial properties, it may be better to refer to the event as a broker reception.

These events can range from relatively simple morning brunches with coffee and bagels to elaborate catered lunches to dinners in restaurants. I have attended receptions for new Class A office spaces that feature musicians and other entertainment. Raffles are also common at these events, as are bonus incentives for fast transactions.

In addition to a marketing kit on the property, each attendee typically receives a gift or a token of the event. One owner, at the start of construction of a new office building, had a reception for local brokers. Upon arrival, each broker received a hard hat to wear and take home; lunch was catered in a large circus tent. Typically, the giveaway items are embossed with a logo for the building or the owner's company. T-shirts, golf shirts, golf balls, scale rulers, and calculators are popular items.

Building receptions are a great way to introduce available space to the brokerage community. The property owner will often pay for this marketing effort.

Communicating with Commercial Brokers

Brokers typically communicate with other commercial practitioners in their area at least monthly, usually circulating a list of their exclusive listings and perhaps some of their customer requirements, seeking co-brokerage assistance to service these clients. For the most part, this is also done electronically as an e-mail attachment. Create address groups on your computer—one with the e-mail addresses of agents in your area—so your message or flyer can instantly reach the entire group. Another broker list might be established for out-of-area brokers, and some investment properties can be marketed to both lists.

Communicating with Customers and Clients

Create several other lists in your address book for your customers and clients. You may want a separate list for investors, developers, and national accounts or wish to segregate groups by size, dollar, or geographic requirements (local, anywhere), etc. Remember when transmitting data via e-mail to send the message to yourself and a blind copy to your list. You probably don't want your clients knowing whom else you are working with.

■ Database Marketing

"Broker is authorized to list the property on any available database." This line appearing in your listing agreement tells property owners that you will be marketing their property on the Internet. You can reinforce this by explaining that you will be placing the listing with various commercial listing services and advertising it in commercial newsgroups, and that these services are national in scope and the property will be seen by potential customers throughout the country. Further, it is important to note that your Internet marketing reaches other brokers and is viewed directly by buyers and sellers.

For a list of commercial real estate Web sites and databases, see the appendix on page 129.

Your Presence on the Web

A personal Web site can be a significant marketing tool, but it shouldn't be boring. Your Web site reflects on you. Care must be taken to develop it properly. People will go to your site out of curiosity, but will they visit it again? Will they contact you because of their visit? Like a newspaper advertisement, the goal is to be contacted. Several things should be included to make your site interesting to them and useful to you:

- Pictures and graphics.
- Frequent display of your phone number and e-mail address. Make it easy for site visitors to contact you (i.e., "click here to e-mail me").

- Your (ever-changing) listings. Be sure to update your site regularly (e.g., "February's Featured Property") or have a link to a listing service.
- Free information. These may be articles the viewer can download, or you may have them request the article via e-mail and then forward it to them. You can write the article or arrange for a local specialist in that field to distribute information for their company. Topics might include the following:
  - Current commercial mortgage terms and rates
  - What you need to know about environmental reports
  - About 1031 exchanges—the basics of investment analysis
  - Send for a free demographics report
- Links to other sites that may be of interest to your customers.
- Perhaps post a monthly newsletter. It can be about local business—who bought what, for how much—publicize your recent deals, provide employment or economic trends, about special funding programs, or even include computer tips. If you create a newsletter, also e-mail it to your address groups. There are organizations and companies that provide monthly newsletters you can send with your name. One example is the Real Estate Cyberspace Society (mentioned in the appendix).

Creativity on the Web

Visualize a customer looking for office space. This customer finds several possible locations on the Internet and e-mails the brokers, who provide various responses. Some brokers text their replies, while others text replies with pictures attached. A few reply with links that take the customer to a video of the property, with an audio description. This is where we are today. Our customers are high tech, and we have the ability to create videos right on our cell phones. However, for marketing purposes, a better grade of camera, one that allows an audio track, is needed. Take a look at YouTube.com, search "property for lease," and consider YouTube.com is another possible marketing outlet. This may not be the best place to advertise your property, but it does give you an idea of the type of video marketing you can create and send to your customers.

QR Codes in Commercial Real Estate

The latest tool in marketing commercial properties is the use of QR codes. **QR codes** have been around for quite a while; they were originally created in 1994 and used to track parts in vehicle manufacturing. Today, they are finding new applications in the marketing of many products. QR codes are matrix barcodes (two-dimensional codes) that can be read by a QR scanner. Mobile technology now allows a smartphone or a mobile phone with a camera to add a QR scanner program and read the QR code (*see* Figure 11.1).

A QR code is simply a bridge to a Web site that, when scanned with a mobile device, takes the consumer directly to that Web site. This QR code takes you to the author's Web site at *www.CommercialEd.com*.

These codes will appear on commercial signs in the future. Think of the possibilities for commercial real estate. The buyer or the tenant is driving around and sees your sign and immediately wants more information. Scanning the QR on your sign takes them to a Web site created specifically for that property, to a link to a full presentation of marketing materials for that building, or to a video journey through the building. The link might also be to the agent's personal Web site, a company Web site, other listings, or just about any URL imaginable.

Figure 11.1 | QR Code Sample

It's important to remember that whatever Web page or site the customer is directed to must be optimized for viewing on a mobile device.

The application is not just for signs. A QR code can be placed on flyers to immediately bring more information to the consumer about that property or the agent. The codes can be used as enhancements on listing presentation materials, taking the customer to the agents for other listings. Some agents are even putting the QR symbol on their cars.

To work with QRs, you need a program to create the QR link and a QR reader application for your mobile device. Just search the Internet and you will find a number of sites to help create your QR symbols and readers—many provide this service without charge. Many people now know of the barcode system, but for the benefit of those who don't, add some small text indicating that a QR reader is required and suggest a site where they can find the reader application.

As mentioned, a great application of this tool is to have the QR take the customer to a video of the property or the agent introducing themselves and their services. Use a QR on your business card and bring the customer to your promotional video. Now, that's a powerful business card!

Social Media

Four different generations of people are living today: seniors or the mature generation (born 1927-1945), baby boomers (born 1946-1964), Generation X (born 1965-1980), and Generation Y or millennials (born 1981-2000), who all communicate differently.

Many clients are computer savvy, but some of senior owners may still prefer postal mail over e-mail. Voicemail messages may be regularly picked up by baby boomers but ignored by younger customers who expect text messaging. Communication is complicated. The best way is to simply ask, "How do you prefer that I contact you?"

Complicating, or complementing, communication is social media. The basic concept of social media is to have conversations online. Some of the more popular applications are Facebook, Twitter, and LinkedIn. On Facebook and Twitter, users share long and short comments about what people are doing or feeling. LinkedIn is more of a business networking site.

There are certainly real estate opportunities in using social media to share listing information, market knowledge, and deal closings. Each social network also has subgroups, some company orientated, others industry related, such as "Commercial Real Estate" on Facebook. LinkedIn, for example, has a "Real Estate Finance and Investment Society" with over 30,000 members.

It's important to ask yourself how much time you have to socialize and what kind of bottom-line results you expect to get. Your answer may be related to your generation. Most commercial agents I know and, more importantly, their clients are boomers or seniors who do not participate in social media networks as much as those from the younger generations. But as time goes on and each generation gets a little older, this might change. The key with any form of marketing is to determine what works for you—what produces the best business results.

E-mail Messages and Signatures

People use e-mail because it is fast, so check your e-mail several times per day and respond to people as quickly as possible. There is a tendency in e-mail messages to be brief and not use complete sentences. Be clear in your messages and be sure to use the spell-checker.

Electronic signatures are available in most e-mail programs. Use this feature to promote yourself or a special property. Once a signature is designed, it's only one or two mouse clicks for that complete message to appear in your e-mail, over and over again. Create several signatures, each for a different purpose. For example, your basic signature may contain your name, phone number, fax number, cell phone number, e-mail address, and Web site. It can also include organizations you belong to or the logos of those groups. Be creative and use color; this is your electronic business card. Design another signature for a featured property or customer requirement. Add it to any e-mail you are sending out.

Property Marketing Plan

Most of what has been discussed in this chapter is essentially a property marketing plan.

To promote a property, use the following tools:

- Signs on the building.
- Local newspaper advertisements (or special papers for larger properties).
- Flyers created for distribution to potential customers or other brokers (via e-mail, fax, or direct mail). Target mailing to specific groups such as doctors in medical buildings. Use the local Yellow Pages or research books in the local library to find addresses. For large projects, purchase mailing lists. Be sure the flyer reflects what information a customer for that type of building will want to know.
- Consider a brokers' reception.
- Property listings placed on all available commercial listing services (Internet).
    - Also use local multiple listing services, if appropriate.
- Property information distributed on all relevant newsgroups.

New Business Marketing Plan

Success in this business requires constant prospecting for new and future business, a high level of organization and record keeping, and consistently working the marketing plan for new business development.

Daily prospecting. Daily prospecting consists of daily mailings to your sphere of influence, follow-up calls, cold calls, and reading for new opportunities. This can be accomplished in 90 minutes per day. This is not consecutive time; the point is to accomplish all three tasks each day.

Begin by creating a sphere-of-influence list of literally everyone you know: friends, relatives, business associates, prior customers, and clients. Then, send an announcement letter that is short and to the point: "I am now in the commercial and investment real estate brokerage business." "I have expanded my business to include commercial and investment real estate brokerage." "Is there anyone you know to whom I may be of service?" You can add a few more lines, but this is the message: we are announcing what we do and asking for a referral. Another tip is that because you are sending this to people you know, include a handwritten postscript that says something like "How are the kids?" "Can't believe it's been two years since I sold you your home!" "How's the golf game?"

The key to this program is the follow-up call. On Monday, you mail four letters; the following Monday, you call each of those four people: "Did you get my letter? Is there anyone you can think of whom I may be able to help?" On Tuesday, mail four more, followed up the next Tuesday. The last thing you say in the brief follow-up conversation is, "I am going to be sending out a newsletter of community news. Can I have your e-mail address?"

Going forward, you can create a quarterly or monthly newsletter and send it to your sphere of influence. It can be fancy—or not. A simple e-mail titled "Community News" that discusses businesses moving in or out of the area, or other community events, is all that is needed. Be sure to conclude with, "By the way, have you thought of anyone I can be of assistance to?"

The next part of daily prospecting is cold calling. Systematically visit every business, office, and industrial building in town. Introduce yourself and make contact with the owner or manager. The goal is to meet every building owner and tenant. Talk about their businesses and, if they are tenants, try to get their lease expiration date. If they are building owners (they invested in the building), be prepared to introduce them to a new investment opportunity. Get their e-mail address and record on your computer what you learned from them; enter their e-mail address in an appropriate address group.

Read the classified ads daily and focus on commercial listings. Most owners of commercial properties are not running for-sale-by-owner ads to avoid paying a commission. Rather, they need to find a tenant to restore their cash flow. Call and list those properties. Also read the trade papers and the legal notices to discover more business opportunities.

Spend 90 minutes prospecting each day. See Figure 11.2 for a proposed schedule.

Figure 11.2 | 90 Minutes of Daily Prospecting

Time	Activity
30 minutes	Send out four announcement letters to people in your sphere-of-influence list. Once set up, this should only require addressing and printing. (10 minutes)
	Follow up with calls to the four letters you sent out this day last week. Did you get my letter? Ask for the referral. (20 minutes)
30 minutes	Visit two buildings (cold call visits), introduce yourself, advise you are in the commercial and investment real estate business, and determine whether the business owner owns the building or leases. Then sell the building owner another investment or obtain the lease expiration date (X-date) if it's a rented space.
30 minutes	Read classified ads, call four ads of space for rent by owner (FSBOs), and start the conversation by offering to sell them another investment property. Also, list at least two of the advertised properties for rent.

Do this five days per week.

Results	Month	Year
Personal contacts of people you know:		
By mail	80	960
By phone	80	960
In person visits with business owners:	40	480
FSBO calls to investors:	80	960
Rental listings	40	480
Total new business opportunities:	380/month	3,840/year

Current activity comes from your sign calls, advertisements, flyers, and properties placed on listing systems. But what happens when you sell or lease those properties? Sometimes an activity (income) lull can occur. To manage your business and have more consistent activity, invest part of your time in developing new business every day. This will result in many future opportunities and more consistent business income.

Building Your Business

We are in the people business. Helping people with their real estate needs is what we do. Advertising and Internet sites are the tools we use to meet people who need our assistance.

Where else can we meet people who may need our services? In most local areas, we find chambers of commerce and service clubs, such as Lions, Rotary, Kiwanis, and others. The members of these groups are local business people, our target customers.

Join these groups in your area. But don't just pay dues. Get involved, go to meetings, and serve on committees; soon, everyone will know who you are and what you do. This is building your future business.

Become the speaker. Most of these groups meet for breakfast, lunch, or dinner, and they typically have a speaker at each meeting. Consider speaking to your group or others you may not be a member of. Bring them up to date on commercial building values in your area, market trends, current financing requirements, the market in general.

Networking

Another way to build your business is by networking, regularly getting together with small or large groups to talk about business. Find a local commercial organization to join.

A leads group consists of eight to ten individuals, each from a different business field. The idea is to get together to exchange information about businesses moving in or out of the community. Only one person from a field is allowed—for example one real estate agent, one attorney, one architect, one accountant, one moving company representative, etc. Rules are established so the group does not become a social club. Each person brings two leads to each meeting, and these are discussed and exchanged. The members then follow up individually. If someone is attending but not bringing leads, they are replaced by someone else from the same industry.

With both of these networking concepts, you may find existing organizations to improve your business relationship. You can also start your own.

■ Conclusion

Real estate follows cycles. Properties go up in value for a significant number of years, but when values get too high, the market crashes. Then values go down. Over the years, we have seen this happen, usually over a ten-year cycle—eight years up and two years down. This last real estate cycle, however, lasted almost 15 years. The recent crash was also fueled by irresponsible mortgage lending and consequently the recovery has taken longer, with more people and businesses adversely affected.

But real estate is cyclical, and in many parts of the country, we are seeing the bottom of the cycle. Prices are starting to stabilize. For commercial real estate, this is an ideal time to invest—prices are at their lowest point in five years. Lending has started again. Underwriting standards are more stringent, but with a reasonable down payment and either good cash flow for investments or a good track record for users, loans are being made.

It is a great time to buy real estate.

Use the tools you learned in this book to develop a successful commercial and investment real estate practice. Good luck!

Review Questions

1. What is the MOST effective way to advertise a building?
   a. Sign on the building
   b. Direct mail
   c. Flyer
   d. Classified ad

2. What is the main purpose of a classified ad?
   a. Sell the property
   b. Lease the property
   c. Make the phone ring
   d. Name recognition

3. Print media can be used to market a property
   a. internationally.
   b. to other industries.
   c. regionally.
   d. all of these.

4. What about a property should never put in a classified ad?
   a. Size
   b. Price
   c. Address
   d. Features

5. A blind copy is used for e-mail broadcasts to
   a. sort the recipients.
   b. select specific recipients.
   c. hide a list of recipients.
   d. return a copy to yourself.

6. Flyers with demographic information on them are usually used to promote
   a. office buildings.
   b. retail properties.
   c. industrial buildings.
   d. all of these.

7. What is the MOST important information that should appear on an investment flyer?
   a. Building size
   b. Building location
   c. Net operating income
   d. Demographics

8. Commercial listing services allow properties to be marketed
   a. nationally.
   b. statewide.
   c. regionally.
   d. locally.

9. What is the primary purpose of a Web site?
   a. To display information
   b. Have people contact you
   c. To sell a building
   d. To entertain customers

10. New business development should be done
    a. weekly.
    b. daily.
    c. monthly.
    d. quarterly.

appendix a

Commercial Real Estate Online Resources

This appendix reviews some of the many Web sites available for promoting commercial real estate. Certain sites are available to list and search for properties at no charge, but many offer additional services on a paid subscription basis. Other sites require membership fees for their use, and almost all sites (even if they are free) require a registration process. Most of these Web sites are searchable by type of property, size, price range, and geography within towns, counties, or states.

■ Web Sites

LoopNet (*www.loopnet.com*) is one of the largest national commercial listing services, currently boasting over 2.7 million visitors per month. It contains hundreds of thousands of commercial and investment property listings. You may search for properties for either sale or lease, with many different criteria to select, and place your listings on the system. Basic service is free but restricted, unless you pay a fee to become a premium member. However, even with the restrictions, there are tremendous inventories you can view immediately. The listings include maps and demographics. The site offers a weekly newsletter to members, has a blog, and provides optional marketing services for a fee.

CoStar Group (*www.costar.com*) is a major database of commercial property information to the trade. It services most major metropolitan city markets and is expanding in some surrounding suburban areas. Details of buildings and their market history are available; the site also produces a variety of comprehensive market reports. This is, however, a members-only fee-for-service site. CoStar also has a public site at *www.showcase.com*, where for a nominal monthly fee, agents can list their properties for public view.

CommercialSource (*www.commercialsource.com*) is a Web site developed by the National Association of REALTORS® (NAR) for commercial properties. It is a huge free database of commercial and investment property listings. You can search and put a basic listing on the site, though it does have enhanced features for a fee. In addition, it provides industry news and listen-and-learn webinars and podcasts.

Property Line (*www.propertyline.com*), from Property Line International, Inc., provides a free service at its site. You may place your listings on the system and search for properties in their significant national inventory. It has over 200,000 commercial real estate professionals as members. It creates (for a fee) electronic, full-color, marketing brochures, which are then broadcast to all members of the service. Additional services are available for a fee.

COMMREX (Commercial Real Estate Exchange) (*www.commrex.com*) is a national commercial property information exchange covering many areas of the country. It has listings in many states that can be searched without cost. For an annual fee, you can put an unlimited amount of listings on the site. It provides broadcast e-mail services and other marketing tools to members for a fee.

Dealmakers.net (*www.dealmakers.net*) is free and nationally lists properties for sale or lease and customer requirements. The format is different from most systems; notices are placed in narrative form. Searches are by property type and geographic location. The site also features forums where properties and other industry information is posted by brokers and principals.

Commercial Investment Multiple Listings Service (CIMLS) (*www.cimls.com*) was established in 2001 and now has over 250,000 members. This national site allows searching and listing of commercial properties without cost. Additional marketing services are available for a fee.

RealUp (*www.realup.com*) is a national site that provides searching and listing of properties for free. Just launched in 2009, it has grown considerably and has partnership with most of the national commercial brokerage firms, whose listings are automatically forwarded to the site. Marketing packages are available for a fee.

■ Newsgroups

Joining a newsgroup allows members to post one e-mail message (advertisement, property listing), which will be automatically sent to all the members of the group. You also receive postings from all the other members. Real estate and related industry information is circulated. This is an excellent way to share listing information.

The following are some newsgroups that are currently free:

- **Yahoo** (*groups.yahoo.com*) has thousands of real estate newsgroups (e.g., 1031 Market, Commercial Property, Investor, Investors, Real Estate, and Real Estate Investor Daily). You sign up for each newsgroup separately and then receive e-mail messages from its members.
- **Dealmakers.net** (*www.dealmakers.net*), as mentioned previously, has excellent free forums. Some of the forums or newsgroups are Commercial, Investment Real Estate, Net Biz For Sale, Property For Lease, ESP Retailing, and Tenant Tip. In particular, I like the Tenant Tips group, where national retailers post when they are looking for space. It includes their criteria and contact information.

These are just a few of the available Web sites where properties can be marketed, or where you can search to find customers' requirements. Learn to use the tools at your disposal.

Organizational Sites

Many real estate organizations have their own Web sites. Some are national, including the examples listed here, but commercial real estate groups exist in many different states and local areas. Search the Internet to find commercial organizations in your area.

Certified Commercial Investment Member (CCIM) Institute (*www.ccim.com*) is an affiliate of the National Association of REALTORS®, the CCIM Institute provides extensive educational courses leading to the CCIM designation.

The Society of Industrial and Office REALTORS® (SIOR) (*www.sior.com*) is also an affiliate of the National Association of REALTORS®. This organization provides educational programs in its area of specialty leading to the SIOR designation.

The **International Council of Shopping Centers** (*www.icsc.org*) site offers information about its organization and retailers. This group has conventions throughout the country during the year. Its largest gathering is in Las Vegas, Nevada, generally in May, where tens of thousands of retailers, developers, and brokers gather to do business.

The **U.S. Green Building Council's** (*www.usgbc.org*) site leads you to green education opportunities, LEED rating systems, resources, news and events, and an opportunity to join local chapters.

Real Estate News

Being on top of real estate news and knowing what is going on in the industry is important to your knowledge as a professional. Subscriptions to e-news about real estate are usually free.

Globe Street (*www.globest.com*) provides daily national and regional real estate news about deals, trends and other industry information. You may sign up for various daily alerts at no cost.

Today's Real Estate Advisor (*www.rismedia.com*) subscribers can receive free daily articles on real estate. Although many of the articles are written to the residential side of the business, many of the tips and concepts can be applied to commercial real estate as well. They do have other services available for a fee.

Inman News (*www.inman.com*) specializes in real estate information and articles. This national paper has a special section just for commercial real estate, but requires a fee for full information.

answer key

Chapter 1: Commercial Real Estate Opportunities

1. **d.** Owners of commercial properties may be individuals or companies.
2. **b.** Third-party advisers influence the owner's decisions.
3. **b.** Most commercial property purchases require 25 to 30 percent down payment.
4. **c.** Bring third-party advisers into the loop as soon as possible.
5. **b.** Several forms are needed to list properties.
6. **c.** Investors plan for disposal of buildings when they are purchased.
7. **d.** Tenant rep agreements define the responsibilities of the tenant and broker.
8. **b.** Commercial customers present opportunities for repeat business.
9. **c.** Every three to five years, businesses change for good or bad.
10. **d.** Almost any commercial property can be an investment.

Chapter 2: All About Office Buildings

1. **c.** Office buildings are categorized Class A, B, or C.
2. **b.** Time lowers a building's classification.
3. **c.** Class C buildings are functional but not impressive.
4. **d.** The more technology capable, the smarter the building.
5. **a.** Rentable square footage is the billable amount.
6. **b.** The loss factor ads common-area space to the rental cost.
7. **c.** The tenant improvement allowance is a predetermined amount of money the landlord will spend to finish the space for the tenant.
8. **d.** Beware a right of first refusal.
9. **d.** The rentable square footage multiplied by the total rent per square foot is the annual rent; this amount divided by 12 months equals the total cost per month.
10. **d.** In NNN leases, the tenant pays all expenses.

Chapter 3: Retail Properties

1. **b.** Anchor tenants draw customers to the site with their advertising.
2. **d.** End caps provide several advantages over stores in the middle of a strip center.
3. **b.** The AM Side represents the morning side of traffic.
4. **b.** Plain vanilla shell construction is not finished.
5. **b.** There may not be sufficient parking to allow certain uses.
6. **c.** Demographic reports help retailers decide on locations.
7. **d.** Percentage leases only apply to retail sales.
8. **c.** Anchor tenants help lease other spaces in the center.
9. **b.** A strip center is a single building divided into 5 to 10 stores.
10. **a.** Knowing what stores are in the area will help market vacant space.

answer key **133**

Chapter 4: Industrial Buildings and Their Physical Characteristics

1. **c.** Under steel is how height is measured in industrial buildings.
2. **a.** Column placement dictates movement within a building.
3. **c.** Tail-boards are often declining ramps to level the truck bed with the building.
4. **d.** Usually 10 percent of an industrial building is office space.
5. **d.** Industrial businesses are high-tech today and require high-speed computer and phone lines.
6. **a.** Research into the history of a property is done in Phase I environmental reports.
7. **d.** Environmental problems can be solved in many ways.
8. **c.** An auto dealership is not a type of building.
9. **d.** A series of forms are necessary to list buildings.
10. **b.** The location of the building on the site helps determine available truck access.

Chapter 5: Introduction to Financial Analysis

1. **d.** Total tenant income considers all three components.
2. **b.** Common-area maintenance (CAM) includes shared services for all the tenants.
3. **a.** Tax escalation clauses require tenants to pay their proportionate share of increases.
4. **d.** Gross leasable area (GLA) is all possible rental space on the property.
5. **c.** Income (affected by vacancy) generally includes CAM and tax escalation income.
6. **d.** Percentages are always used to calculate vacancy and management expense and generally used to calculate repair and maintenance.
7. **b.** Total gross income minus total operating expenses equals net operating income.
8. **d.** Other income sources are not affected by tenants.
9. **b.** All figures must be converted to annual income or expense.
10. **a.** An Investment Analysis Worksheet is a tool to gather the data necessary for financial analysis.

Chapter 6: The Value of Investments

1. **b.** Leveraging is defined as the use of borrowed funds to finance a portion of the cost of an investment.
2. **b.** Cash-on-cash = CFBT ÷ Initial investment.
3. **c.** CFBT = Net operating income – Annual debt service.
4. **d.** Internal rate of return (IRR) considers the entire holding period of an investment.
5. **a.** The capitalization rate is the desired profit percentage of investors.
6. **d.** NOI – Annual debt service = CFBT.
7. **d.** The interest rate and terms of the mortgage affect the cash-on-cash return.
8. **b.** Here, the CAP rate formula is used to determine the return on investment.
   NOI ÷ Value = CAP (ROI)
   $67,500 (NOI) ÷ $450,000 (Value) = 0.15; 15% return on investment.

9. b. To calculate cash-on-cash return, one must first calculate cash flow before taxes (CFBT). NOI − Annual debt service = CFBT
$67,500 (NOI) − $38,934 (Debt Service) = $28,566 (CFBT)
CFBT ÷ Initial investment = Cash-on-cash return
$$\frac{\$28{,}566 \text{ (CFBT)}}{\$100{,}000 \text{ (initial investment)}} = 0.2857; 29\% \text{ cash-on-cash return}$$

10. b. $$\frac{\$28{,}566 \text{ (CFBT)}}{\$200{,}000 \text{ (initial investment)}} = 0.1428; 14\% \text{ cash-on-cash return}$$

Because calculators automatically round off, it is suggested you calculate using four digits.

Chapter 7: Forecasting Cash Flows

1. b. The higher the CAP rate desired, the less an investor will pay for a property.
2. a. The cash-on-cash return reflects the owner's (seller's) return based on down payment and financing.
3. d. Market value can be determined by three different methods; it is best to consider all three when pricing a property.
4. d. A buyer will question all assumptions and verify all information.
5. c. Management fees are typically a percentage of the rent roll.
6. d. Repair and maintenance expenses may be calculated as a percentage of gross operating income, potential rental income, or a specific dollar amount.
7. a. If the buyer and the seller can agree on the percentage adjustments for vacancy, repair, and management, the price will be narrowed for final negotiations.
8. c. Projections of income, expense, and NOI are used to calculate current and future market value.
9. c. Leveraging implies a mortgage in lieu of an all-cash purchase reducing the amount of the initial investment to a down payment.
10. d. The NOI used in conjunction with the investors desired CAP rate will determine the buyer's value of the property.

Chapter 8: Depreciation and Cash Flow After Taxes

1. b. Depreciation is taken on commercial and investment properties, never the owner's personal residence. Land does not depreciate.
2. b. Commercial buildings are depreciated over 39 years. Residential investment buildings are depreciated over 27.5 years.
3. d. Currently 39 years, this is a category that has changed depreciation periods recently; always check with a tax advisor for current updates.
4. b. Cost segregation may provide shorter depreciation periods for personal property in a building and land improvements.
5. d. In calculating taxable income, operating expenses, mortgage interest on loans, and depreciation may be deducted from the gross income.
6. c. Unused repair and maintenance funds must be added to the NOI before calculating income taxes.
7. a. Dividing the cash flow after taxes (CFAT) by the initial investment determines the return on equity.
8. c. The return on investment is determined by dividing the cash flow after taxes (CFAT) by the purchase price.
9. d. The current marginal tax brackets are scheduled to expire on December 31, 2012.
10. a. $47,000 multiplied by 28 percent equals $13,160, the income tax due.

Chapter 9: Selling Property: Capital Gains Taxes and 1031 Exchanges

1. **d.** Capital gains taxes are applicable to all real estate sales.
2. **b.** The IRS provides a residential exclusion; homeowners may exclude the first $250,000 in gain ($500,000 if married and filing jointly) on the sale of one home every two years. (Other conditions apply.)
3. **d.** The depreciation recapture tax rate is currently 25 percent.
4. **b.** Currently, if the taxpayer's marginal tax rate is above the 15 percent income bracket, the capital gains tax on appreciation would be 15 percent. However, since 2008, when the taxpayer is in the 15 percent income bracket or below, the current tax is zero percent. These tax rates are scheduled to expire on December 31, 2012.
5. **d.** There is currently no licensing required for qualified intermediaries.
6. **a.** A 1031 exchange defers the capital gains taxes to the property being acquired.
7. **d.** The IRS prohibits the taxpayer's accountant, attorney, or real estate agent from serving as the qualified intermediary, if the taxpayer has done business with them in the last two years.
8. **d.** For a full deferral of capital gains taxes, three components must be *equal to or greater than* value, equity, and debt.
9. **c.** 1031 exchanges are time sensitive. The entire process must be completed within 180 days.
10. **a.** In a 1031 exchange, the property to be acquired must be declared within 45 days.

Chapter 10: Dealing with Other Brokers

1. **d.** Commission splits are negotiated based on market conditions.
2. **c.** Override commissions allow maximum promotion of properties to other brokers.
3. **b.** Showing a customer many properties; working with a customer extensively is known as "running" the customer.
4. **d.** Referral fees may be negotiated in many different ways.
5. **a.** The listing agent controls the terms offered to co-broke a property.
6. **c.** Co-broke agreements define the way a listing is managed, as directed by the property owner.
7. **c.** Registering potential customers with owners helps protect brokers against a customer attempting to circumvent the broker.
8. **b.** All the potential parties to the transaction sign the agreement.
9. **c.** By recording the customers who have viewed a property, a notice of showing form demonstrates activity to owners.
10. **b.** Written notices may provide the best document trail.

Chapter 11: Marketing for Success

1. **a.** Business owners often visit areas they are considering locating to.
2. **c.** An ad is a tool to meet new customers.
3. **d.** Many forms of print media may be useful in promoting commercial properties.
4. **c.** Ads should cause a customer to meet with the broker to see the property.
5. **c.** E-mail provides the ability to send a group a message without revealing the other recipients.
6. **b.** Retailers base site selection on demographic information.
7. **c.** Flyers should contain the information that those who would be interested in that type of property would want to know.

8. **a.** Through commercial listing services, marketing can be done with virtually no geographic bounds.
9. **b.** Web sites are advertisements that cause customers to call you.
10. **b.** New business development should be a consistent daily effort.

glossary

1031 exchange a method that allows the seller of real estate to defer the capital gains taxes on that sale of a property by buying another real estate property. Many rules apply.

additional rent a pass-through to the tenants of certain building expenses in addition to the base rent they pay.

add-on factor a percentage representing the common areas of a building. It is also a type of formula used to determine how much space a tenant must pay for.

adjusted basis as used in calculating capital gains taxes, is the original cost or basis plus certain additions and minus certain deductions. An increase in basis will reduce the taxable gain.

anchor tenant household-name store (often a supermarket, department store, or national chain store) that draws people to the store and consequently to the shopping center. The anchor store usually does extensive advertising, which effectively benefits all the tenants of the center.

annual debt service cost required to repay principle and interest on a mortgage loan each year.

annual property operating data (APOD) an investment analysis worksheet developed by the CCIM Institute.

as-built a floor plan that specifies existing construction within a unit (i.e., walls of private offices, conference rooms).

assumption agreement type of document that protects a broker's possible future commission, due from lease options, in the event the property is sold.

basis as used in calculating capital gains taxes, is usually the original cost of the property.

build to suit constructing a building per the tenant's or buyer's plans and specifications.

capital gains taxes tax on profit realized from the sale of any capital investment including real estate.

cash flow before taxes (CFBT) net operating income (NOI) less the annual debt service equals cash flow before taxes (referring to income taxes).

cash flow after taxes (CFAT) annual income received from investment property, which is subject to income tax. You may deduct from that gross income the operating expenses of the property, real estate property taxes, interest on mortgage loans, and depreciation. The remaining net income is taxed at the taxpayer's marginal tax rate. What remains after payment of income taxes is the cash flow after taxes (CFAT).

cash-on-cash return a simple return measure. Calculated as cash flow before taxes (CFBT) divided by the initial investment.

capitalization (CAP) rate a percentage representing a rate of return on an real estate investment.

ceiling height in industrial buildings, the ceiling height is measured from the floor to the bottom of the girders that hold up the roof.

co-broke agreements written agreements between the brokers. Considerable real estate brokerage business is done with one firm representing the selling or landlord side of the transaction and another firm representing the buyer or tenant, necessitating written agreements.

column span in an industrial building, the distance between the columns.

commission overrides sometimes provided by listing agreements obtained from property owners. This in essence, allows the listing broker to market the property to other brokers offering a full commission. This added incentive to the brokerage community helps promote the property.

common-area maintenance (CAM) services provided to all the tenants in the building (i.e. rubbish collection, landscaping, window washing, etc.). A landlord may enter into various contracts for these services, and the costs are then proportionately bill to each tenant as additional rent.

comparable sales approach determining the value of a property by comparing it to recent sales of similar properties.

cost approach determining the value of a property based on what it would cost to construct the same building today.

cost segregation an accounting method that provides shorter depreciation time periods for personal property (5 years or 7 years) and for land improvements (15 years) resulting in higher depreciation in the early years of owning a building.

demographics statistics showing total population, median income, ages, and other data within circles drawn around a site (typically 1, 3 and 5 miles).

depreciation (cost recovery) under rules established by the IRS, owners of commercial or investment property depreciate buildings for estimated wear, tear, and obsolescence. Specific rules apply.

depreciation recapture tax a capital gains tax on commercial and investment property.

end cap In a strip of stores, the two stores on either end of the center. The locations afford those tenants visibility (advertising) on two sides or a possible drive-through window.

environmental reports results of an examination and inspection of a property to determine the presence of any contamination. They are generally called Phase 1, Phase 2, and Phase 3 reports.

equity the value of one's interest in the property, consisting of fair market value less any outstanding debt or other encumbrances. Equity generally increases as the mortgage balance decreases.

exit strategy to determine in advance how long a property will be held before it is sold and projecting the overall return on that investment.

income approach determining the value of a property by analyzing the cash flow and using a capitalization rate formula.

initial investment when financing the purchase of a property, the down payment, which may include the acquisition costs.

internal rate of return (IRR) a calculation that covers the entire life of the investment and in essence shows the average annual return for the entire holding period. This mathematically complex calculation is the discount rate at which the present value of future cash flows is exactly equal to the initial capital investment.

lease extract a summary of the leases in a building showing commencement and ending dates, escalations, current rent, additional rent, and options.

leverage the use of borrowed funds to finance a portion of the cost of an investment.

loading dock raised platforms, usually outside of the building, that bring the bay of the truck body level with the floor of the building. The goods can then be easily rolled off the truck.

loss or core factor a percentage representing the common areas in a building. This is also a type of formula used to determine how much space a tenant must pay for.

net operating income (NOI) a measure of a property's financial performance, expressed in dollars; in the simplest sense, the gross income less owner's operating expenses equals the NOI.

net or usable square footage the space in a building that a tenant has exclusive use of.

Noncircumvention and Nondisclosure Agreement A document that originates with the property seller and is signed by the buyer and their representative (broker) indicating that information about the property is proprietary. The information the customer will receive about the property is confidential and may not be shared with other parties with the exception of partners, directors, key employees, or related parties (i.e., attorney or accountant) on a need-to-know basis. It also states that no one signing the agreement may circumvent any other party to the agreement, which helps protect the brokers' commissions.

notice of showing a form or letter advising property owners that their property was introduced to a prospective buyer or tenant, and naming that customer or company.

overhead door refers to garage doors of the type you may have at home, but large enough to allow trucks to actually drive into the building.

percentage lease a form of lease that is exclusive to retail, in which tenants pay a percentage of their sales as part of their rent.

plain vanilla shell a term referring to delivering a building with only the basic walls, roof, and floor constructed; the tenant or buyer would finish the interior construction.

potential rental income reflects the potential income from the entire rentable square footage of the building. There are three components: the actual rent, a projection of income from any temporally unoccupied space, and any additional rent the landlord charges the tenants.

pro forma an analysis showing the financial performance of a property in the current year.

QR code a bridge to a Web site that when scanned with a mobile device takes the consumer directly to that site.

rate of return percentage return on each dollar invested, also known as the yield.

rentable or gross or billable square footage the space in a building that a tenant must pay for. This includes net or usable square footage plus the proportionate share of the building's common areas.

replacement reserves a contingency fund for catastrophic events that would require immediate repair or replacement.

return on equity a percentage representing a return based on after-tax dollars compared to the initial investment.

return on investment (ROI) a percentage representing a rate of return on an all-cash investment.

right of first refusal (ROFR) a lease clause, providing that if an owner decides to sell the property and obtains an offer to purchase the property, a tenant with a right of first refusal may purchase the property. But the tenant must match that offer in dollars and terms exactly.

spreadsheet as used in financial analysis, a projection of a building's financial performance in future years, typically a five- or ten-year analysis.

tail-board an opening into a building, the size of the back of a truck, which is elevated or appears as a declining ramp, so the floor of the building, will be at the height of the bay of the truck; allowing the goods to be rolled off the truck into the building.

tax escalation clause a clause in a lease that states the landlord will pay the real estate taxes on a building as they exist on the day of the lease signing. If, however, the taxes go up after the lease commencement, the tenant will pay a proportionate share of the increase.

tenant improvement allowance when offering space for rent, an offer made by landlords of a specific amount of money they will provide for a new tenant's desired improvements (construction). This may be a fixed sum or based on a dollar value per square foot.

tenant mix determining what types of business are in a group of stores or general area. The focus is to determine what type of business is missing for marketing purposes.

triple net (NNN) lease a form of lease that indicates the tenant will be responsible for paying all the operating expenses of the property.

upside potential evaluation of an investment based on future events that would cause an increase in rents or a reduction of expenses.

workletter a specific description of construction being requested.

index

SYMBOLS
95 percent exception, 102
100 percent rule, 102
1031 exchange, 101

A
Accommodator, 101
Accountant, 10
Acquisition rules, 102
Activity reports, 111
Additional rent, 22
Add-on factor, 20
Adjusted basis, 97, 99
Adjustments, 91
Advertising, 118
After tax cash flow (ATCF), 91
All-cash purchase, 61
AM side, 32
Anchor tenant, 31
Ancillary services, 18
Annual property operating data (APOD), 63, 64
As-built, 21
Assignment, 23
Assumption agreement, 23

B
Basis, 97
Billable square footage, 19, 20
BOMA (Building Owners and Managers Association), 19
Boot, 102
Breakeven point, 37
Broker agreement, 8
Broker cooperation agreement, 110
Broker open house, 120
Building
    commercial, 2
    industrial, 41
    office, 16
    retail, 31
    size, 41
Build to suit, 8
Business cycle, 3
Business style, 84
Buyer perspective, 83

C
Capital gains tax
    calculation, 100
    commercial building, 99
    definition, 97
    personal residence, 97, 98
Capitalization (CAP) rate
    explanation of, 6
    formula, 7
    investment analysis, 73
Capital losses, 97
Cash boot, 103
Cash business, 34
Cash flow, 67
Cash flow after taxes (CFAT)
    calculation, 92
    definition, 91
Cash flow before taxes (CFBT)
    definition, 61
    example, 78, 79
    formula, 62
    investment analysis, 73, 79
Cash-on-cash return
    definition, 61
    formula, 62
    investment analysis, 73
    office building, 80
CCIM (Certified Commercial Investment Member), 63
Ceiling height, 42
Certified Commercial Investment Member (CCIM) Institute, 131
Class A office building, 16
Class B office building, 16
Class C office building, 17
Classified advertising, 119
Clear span, 42
Co-brokerage
    agreement, 108
    open nonexclusive listing, 109
Cold calling, 125
Column spans, 42
Commercial brokerage, 86
Commercial buildings, 2
Commercial flyers, 119
Commercial Investment Multiple Listings Service (CIMLS), 130
Commercial property
    capital gains tax, 99
    inventory, 13
    QR code, 122
    sale of, 98
    types of, 2
CommercialSource, 129
Commission, 106
Common area, 19
Common-area maintenance (CAM), 22
COMMREX, 130
Communication, 121
Comparable sales approach, 82
Computers, 18
Confidentiality clause, 8
Construction, 21
Core factor, 19
Cost approach, 82
CoStar Group, 129
Cost recovery, 89
Cost segregation, 90
Cubic capacity, 42
Current year analysis, 67
Customer/client
    communication, 121
    types of, 3

D
Daily prospecting, 125, 126
Database marketing, 121
Dealmakers.net, 130
Demographics, 35
Depreciation
    definition, 89
    example, 90
    facts, 89
Depreciation recapture tax, 97, 99
Developers, 8
Documentation, 12

E
Effective rent, 5
Electric capacity, 43
Electronic signature, 124
E-mail, 124
End cap, 32
Environmental issues, 44
Environmental report, 44
Equity, 61
Exit strategy, 5
Expenses
    annual cost, 53
    investment analysis, 78

F
Far corner, 33
Feet under steel, 42
Financial analysis, 54
Financing programs, 11

Finishing space, 33
Floor drains, 44
Floor plan, 21, 43
Flyers, 119
Follow-up call, 125

G
Gas station, 34
Globe Street, 131
Gross leasable area (GLA), 22
Gross operating income, 51, 77
Gross square footage, 19, 20

H
Heating, ventilating, air conditioning (HVAC), 43
Highest and best use, 34
Hours, 18

I
Income approach, 6, 82
Industrial property
    building types, 46
    checklist, 46, 47, 48
    marketing, 45
    site inspections, 41
Initial investment, 61
Inman News, 131
Internal rate of return (IRR), 61
International Council of Shopping Centers, 131
Internet, 118
    creativity, 122
    personal web site, 121
Investment
    analysis worksheet, 51, 52, 57, 58, 72
    clients, 5
    methods, 61
    office building as, 24
    property sale, 98
    strategies, 61, 63
    terms, 61
Investor
    strategies, 63

L
Lease
    assignment, 23
    clauses, 21
    definition, 21
    escalations, 24
    expirations, 24
    extract, 67, 68
    notes, 74
    restaurant, 34
    restrictions, 35
    retail, 35
    terms/increases, 75

Leasehold improvements, 90
Legal representation, 10
Leverage, 61
Leveraged purchase, 61
Like kind, 101
Listing information checklist, 11, 12
Loading docks, 42
Location, 35
Long-term capital gains, 97
LoopNet, 129
Loss factor, 19

M
Mall, 31
Management expenses, 85
Marketing plan, 124, 125
Market value
    buyer's perspective, 85
    calculation, 54, 57
    formula, 7
    investment analysis, 81
    projected, 81
    seller's perspective, 85
Matrix barcode, 122
Medical office space, 17
Mixed-use buildings, 90
Mortgage boot, 103

N
National Association of REALTORS®, 13
Neighborhood center, 31
Net operating income (NOI)
    calculation, 57
    definition, 5
    formula, 5
    investment analysis, 53, 71, 79
Net profit, 99
Net square footage, 19
Networking, 127
New business marketing plan, 125
Newsgroups, 130
Newsletter, 125
Non-Circumvention and Nondisclosure Agreement
    proprietary info, 111
    sample, 112, 113
    use of, 109
Notice of showing, 115

O
Observation period, 34
Office building
    as investment, 24
    cash-on-cash return, 80
    checklist, 25, 26, 27
    classification, 16
    construction, 16
    current year analysis, 67, 68

    investment analysis, 74, 75
    market value, 81
    parking requirements, 18
Office space, 43
Online resources, 129
Open house, 120
Open nonexclusive listing, 109
Operating expense
    calculation of, 56
    investment analysis worksheet, 71
Option to buy, 23
Organizational sites, 131
Other income, 51, 70, 77
Outlet center, 31
Out parcels, 31
Overhead doors, 42
Ownership information, 9

P
Pad sites, 31
Parking, 18
Partial demographic report, 36
Partial exchange, 102
Percentage lease, 35, 37
Permitted business use, 35
Phase III inspection, 45
Phase II inspection, 45
Phase I inspection, 44
Phones, 18
Plain vanilla shell, 33
Potential rental income
    calculation of, 54
    investment analysis, 77
    spreadsheet, 74
Power centers, 32
Prequalification, 11
Press release, 119
Primary/principal residence, 97
Print media, 118
Pro forma, 51, 84
Projected rent, 55
Property Line, 130
Property marketing plan, 124
Prospecting, 125, 126

Q
QR code
    definition, 122
    sample, 123
Qualified intermediary (QI), 101
Qualified properties, 101, 102

R
Rate of return, 61
Real estate news, 131
Records, 111
Referral agreements, 106, 107
Refrigeration, 44

Regional shopping center, 31
Rentable square footage, 19, 20
Rent per month, 28
Rent per square foot, 28
Rent roll, 24, 55, 70
Repairs/maintenance
    contingency, 83
    evaluation, 85
    expense calculation, 78
Replacement reserves, 53
Restaurants, 33
Retail property
    building, 31
    building checklist, 37, 38
    lease, 35
    site considerations, 34
    specialty business, 33
    terms, 32
    zoning, 34
Return on equity, 93
Return on investment (ROI)
    all-cash purchase, 93
    illustration, 6
    investment analysis, 80
    user investors, 4
Revenue Act of 1918, 101
Right of first refusal (ROFR) clause, 24

S
Shopping center, 31
Short-term capital gains, 97
Showing record
    purpose of, 114
    sample, 115
Signs, 118
Site inspections, 41
Site plan, 41
Social media, 123
Society of Industrial and Office REALTORS (SIOR), 131
Space, 19
Specialty business, 33
Sphere-of-influence list, 125
Spreadsheet, 74
Sprinklers, 43
Straight-line depreciation method, 89
Strip center, 31

T
Tail-boards, 43
Tax escalation
    calculation, 23
    clause, 22
Tax expense, 78
Tax Relief, Unemployment Insurance Reauthorization and Job Creation Act, 90
Technical services, 43
Tenant
    improvement allowance, 21
    income, 51, 70
    mix, 32, 37
Tenant-buyer representatives, 8
Tenant-occupied unit square footage, 19
Third-party advisers, 9
Three-investment property rule, 102
Today's Real Estate Advisor, 131
Total expenses, 79
Total gross income, 71
Total operating expenses, 53
Traffic counts, 35
Triple-net lease (NNN)
    office buildings, 24
    retail property, 32
Truck access, 41
Turnkey, 34

U
Underwriting standards, 11
Upside potential, 67, 79
Usable square footage, 19
User customers, 3
User investor
    purchase terms, 5
    return on investment, 4
U.S. Green Buildings Council, 131
Utilities, 18

V
Vacancy adjustment
    investment analysis, 77
    rate, 83, 85
Vacancy contingency, 51, 55

W
Website
    commercial inventory, 13
    personal, 121
    resources, 129
Workletter, 21

Y
Yahoo, 130